Antidepressants

Other books in the At Issue series:

At ✹ Issue

Antidepressants

Katherine Read Dunbar, *Book Editor*

Bruce Glassman, *Vice President*
Bonnie Szumski, *Publisher*
Helen Cothran, *Managing Editor*

GREENHAVEN PRESS
An imprint of Thomson Gale, a part of The Thomson Corporation

THOMSON
✷
™
GALE

Detroit • New York • San Francisco • San Diego • New Haven, Conn.
Waterville, Maine • London • Munich

For more information, contact
Greenhaven Press
27500 Drake Rd.
Farmington Hills, MI 48331-3535
Or you can visit our Internet site at http://www.gale.com

LIBRARY OF CONGRESS CATALOGING-IN-PUBLICATION DATA	
Antidepressants / Katherine Read Dunbar, book editor.	
p. cm. — (At issue)	
Includes bibliographical references and index.	
ISBN 0-7377-3115-X (lib. : alk. paper) — ISBN 0-7377-3116-8 (pbk. : alk. paper)	
1. Antidepressants—Popular works. 2. Depression, Mental—Popular works.	
I. Dunbar, Katherine. II. At issue (San Diego, Calif.)	
RM332.A5733 2006	
615'.78—dc22	2005040330

Printed in the United States of America

Contents

Introduction

In June 2003 the Museum of Modern Art in New York was flooded with doctors from all around the United States. These doctors were not attending a convention, however, but an extravagant party put on by Pfizer, one of the pharmaceutical giants and the maker of Prozac, a popular antidepressant. The pharmaceutical company wined and dined this elite group of doctors, who were given an all-expense paid trip to New York City. All in attendance were showered with gifts, dinners, and offers of trips to desired locations. "The company called it an honorarium," says Rudy Mueller, an upstate New York doctor. However, in reality, he argues, "It's bribery. This is very effective marketing." Every year the pharmaceutical industry invests millions of dollars on the marketing of antidepressants to doctors. Whether or not this has an impact on the prescription of these drugs is hotly debated.

Some people claim that heavy marketing by drug companies has a strong influence on doctors' decisions about whether to prescribe antidepressants, and which antidepressants are prescribed. They point out that the number of antidepressant prescriptions written by doctors annually has been rising. Visits from drug representatives to physicians and psychiatrists have been increasing steadily, with psychiatrists as one of the most aggressively targeted groups. According to author Elizabeth Fried Ellen, in 1999 alone drug companies spent more than $335 million on marketing directed at psychiatrists.

Critics claim that during these visits, drug companies overwhelm doctors with gifts, expensive dinners, and free trips to exotic locations. Many doctors are uncomfortable with the amount of marketing done by drug companies and the possible impact this has on them. For example, Galen Stahle, a Minneapolis-area psychiatrist, writes millions of dollars worth of prescriptions every year. After one psychiatric convention where he was offered a trip to Hawaii, Stahle voiced his fear about the effect these gifts may be having on doctors. "I don't know if it's short of bribery, or if it is bribery," he commented. Says Arnold Relman, a Harvard Medical School professor, "I think it's sleaze. . . . Anybody who's been in that position knows that yes, those gifts, $60, $100, $40, again and again, do influence your attitude about that company and will influence the prescriptions that you write."

Doctors do receive the majority of their information about antidepressants from drug companies; however, this information is widely regarded as biased, and many people fear that doctors are writing prescriptions based on incomplete or incorrect information. Critics allege that drug representatives overstate the effectiveness of their drugs, often promoting uses not approved by the Food and Drug Administration. Many people point out that if drug representatives do in fact influence doctors' prescribing habits then patients suffer because the best and most effective drugs are not necessarily the ones being promoted. Shannon Brownlee, a senior fellow at the New America Foundation, says, "The corrupting influence of the pharmaceutical industry money has hurt patients."

Still, many doctors hold to the belief that the gifts offered by drug companies have no effect on their prescribing of antidepressants. Jeffrey Bedrick, a psychiatrist at Mount Sinai Medical Center in New York City, believes that he can see the bias of the drug companies and filter it out. Although he turns down the fancy dinners, he says that he enjoys going to the lectures these companies offer because he finds them interesting. Ronald Ruden, a New York City internist, laughs at the idea of being influenced by the free dinners drug representatives offer. "I mean, I can afford to go any place I want," he says. Many doctors see the gifts as perks of the job, not as bribery or attempts to influence their behavior. Jodi Star, a graduating psychiatrist resident from the University of Cincinnati says that she appreciates the free samples given to her by drug companies. However, she adds, "I can take everything they say with a grain of salt, because we've learned these skills." Like Star, many doctors feel that they have been trained to take in information and see beyond the biases, thus allowing them not to be influenced.

Despite the possible biases of drug companies, many doctors feel that drug representatives are a valuable and much needed source of information about antidepressants. One Manhattan psychiatrist contends that he has "learned a ton from drug reps and their educational programs." Very often doctors simply do not have the time to do their own research on antidepressants, and they feel that the knowledge drug companies give them is invaluable. Benjamin Crocker, a Maine psychiatrist, feels that drug representatives can be an important resource for doctors. "Reps can teach docs to be more careful," he maintains, "and more aware of side effects."

Pharmaceutical companies spend huge sums of money each year marketing antidepressants. Clearly, the question of whether this practice has a negative impact on doctors is highly controversial. Moreover, as the prescribing of antidepressants increases, the controversy continues to heat up.

1

Overview: Antidepressants

National Institute of Mental Health

The National Institute of Mental Health is the lead federal agency for research on mental and behavioral disorders.

Major depression is a condition that lasts for a period of two weeks or more and inhibits a person's ability to lead a normal life. People with major depression can, however, benefit greatly from treatment with antidepressant medication. There are various antidepressants, each with different types of side effects. Older antidepressants such as tricyclic antidepressants and monoamine oxidase inhibitors are effective but can have more dangerous side effects if they are not used properly. The newest class of antidepressants, called selective serotonin reuptake inhibitors, work as well as the older ones but have fewer side effects.

Major depression, the kind of depression that will most likely benefit from treatment with medications, is more than just "the blues." It is a condition that lasts 2 weeks or more, and interferes with a person's ability to carry on daily tasks and enjoy activities that previously brought pleasure. Depression is associated with abnormal functioning of the brain. An interaction between genetic tendency and life history appears to determine a person's chance of becoming depressed. Episodes of depression may be triggered by stress, difficult life events, side effects of medications, or medication/substance withdrawal, or even viral infections that can affect the brain.

National Institute of Mental Health, "Antidepressant Medications," www.nimh. nih.gov, 2002.

Depressed people will seem sad, or "down," or may be unable to enjoy their normal activities. They may have no appetite and lose weight (although some people eat more and gain weight when depressed). They may sleep too much or too little, have difficulty going to sleep, sleep restlessly, or awaken very early in the morning. They may speak of feeling guilty, worthless, or hopeless; they may lack energy or be jumpy and agitated. They may think about killing themselves and may even make a suicide attempt. Some depressed people have delusions (false, fixed ideas) about poverty, sickness, or sinfulness that are related to their depression. Often feelings of depression are worse at a particular time of day, for instance, every morning or every evening.

Treating Depression

Not everyone who is depressed has all these symptoms, but everyone who is depressed has at least some of them, co-existing, on most days. Depression can range in intensity from mild to severe. Depression can co-occur with other medical disorders such as cancer, heart disease, stroke, Parkinson's disease, Alzheimer's disease, and diabetes. In such cases, the depression is often overlooked and is not treated. If the depression is recognized and treated, a person's quality of life can be greatly improved.

Antidepressants are used most often for serious depressions, but they can also be helpful for some milder depressions. Antidepressants are not "uppers" or stimulants, but rather take away or reduce the symptoms of depression and help depressed people feel the way they did before they became depressed.

> *Major depression, the kind of depression that will most likely benefit from treatment with medications, is more than just 'the blues.'*

The doctor chooses an antidepressant based on the individual's symptoms. Some people notice improvement in the first couple of weeks; but usually the medication must be taken regularly for at least 6 weeks and, in some cases, as many as 8 weeks before the full therapeutic effect occurs. If there is little or no change in symptoms after 6 or 8 weeks, the doctor may prescribe a different medication or add a second medication such as [the mood stabilizer] lithium, to augment the action of the original antidepressant. Because there is no way of knowing beforehand which medication will be effective, the doctor may have to prescribe first one and then another. To give a medication time to be effective and to prevent a relapse of the depression once the patient is responding to an antidepressant, the medication should be continued for 6 to 12 months, or in some cases longer, carefully following the doctor's instructions. When a patient and the doctor feel that medications can be discontinued, withdrawal should be discussed as to how best to taper off the medication gradually. Never discontinue medication without talking to the doctor about it. For those who have had several bouts of depression, long-term treatment with medication is the most effective means of preventing more episodes.

The past decade has seen the introduction of many new antidepressants that work as well as the older ones but have fewer side effects.

Dosage of antidepressants varies, depending on the type of drug and the person's body chemistry, age, and, sometimes, body weight. Traditionally, antidepressant dosages are started low and raised gradually over time until the desired effect is reached without the appearance of troublesome side effects. Newer antidepressants may be started at or near therapeutic doses.

Early Antidepressants

From the 1960s through the 1980s, tricyclic antidepressants (named for their chemical structure) were the first line of treatment for major depression. Most of these medications affected two chemical neurotransmitters, norepinephrine and serotonin.[1] Though the tricyclics are as effective in treating depression as the newer antidepressants, their side effects are usually more unpleasant; thus, today tricyclics such as imipramine, amitriptyline,

1. Neurotransmitters are chemicals in the brain that facilitate communication between nerve cells. An inadequate amount of these can cause depression. Antidepressants relieve depression by increasing the amount of these neurotransmitters.

nortriptyline, and desipramine are used as a second- or third-line treatment. Other antidepressants introduced during this period were monoamine oxidase inhibitors (MAOIs). MAOIs are effective for some people with major depression who do not respond to other antidepressants. They are also effective for the treatment of panic disorder and bipolar depression. MAOIs approved for the treatment of depression are phenelzine (Nardil), tranyl-cypromine (Parnate), and isocarboxazid (Marplan). Because substances in certain foods, beverages, and medications can cause dangerous interactions when combined with MAOIs, people on these agents must adhere to dietary restrictions. This has deterred many clinicians and patients from using these effective medications, which are in fact quite safe when used as directed.

A New Class of Antidepressants

The past decade [1990s] has seen the introduction of many new antidepressants that work as well as the older ones but have fewer side effects. Some of these medications primarily affect one neurotransmitter, serotonin, and are called selective serotonin reuptake inhibitors (SSRIs). These include fluoxetine (Prozac), sertraline (Zoloft), fluvoxamine (Luvox), paroxetine (Paxil), and citalopram (Celexa).

The late 1990s ushered in new medications that, like the tricyclics, affect both norepinephrine and serotonin but have fewer side effects. These new medications include venlafaxine (Effexor) and nefazadone (Serzone). . . .

Other newer medications chemically unrelated to the other antidepressants are the sedating mirtazepine (Remeron) and the more activating bupropion (Wellbutrin). Wellbutrin has not been associated with weight gain or sexual dysfunction but is not used for people with, or at risk for, a seizure disorder.

Side Effects of Tricyclic Antidepressants

Each antidepressant differs in its side effects and in its effectiveness in treating an individual person, but the majority of people with depression can be treated effectively by one of these antidepressants. . . .

Antidepressants may cause mild, and often temporary, side effects (sometimes referred to as adverse effects) in some people. Typically, these are not serious. However, any reactions or side effects that are unusual, annoying, or that interfere with functioning should be reported to the doctor immediately. The most common side effects of tricyclic antidepressants, and ways to deal with them, are as follows:

- *Dry mouth*—it is helpful to drink sips of water; chew sugarless gum; brush teeth daily.
- *Constipation*—bran cereals, prunes, fruit, and vegetables should be in the diet.
- *Bladder problems*—emptying the bladder completely may be difficult, and the urine stream may not be as strong as usual. Older men with enlarged prostate conditions may be at particular risk for this problem. The doctor should be notified if there is any pain.
- *Sexual problems*—sexual functioning may be impaired; if this is worrisome, it should be discussed with the doctor.
- *Blurred vision*—this is usually temporary and will not necessitate new glasses. Glaucoma patients should report any change in vision to the doctor.
- *Dizziness*—rising from the bed or chair slowly is helpful.
- *Drowsiness as a daytime problem*—this usually passes soon. A person who feels drowsy or sedated should not drive or operate heavy equipment. The more sedating antidepressants are generally taken at bedtime to help sleep and to minimize daytime drowsiness.
- *Increased heart rate*—pulse rate is often elevated. Older patients should have an electrocardiogram (EKG) before beginning tricyclic treatment.

Side Effects of Newer Antidepressants

The newer antidepressants, including SSRIs, have different types of side effects, as follows:

- *Sexual problems*—fairly common, but reversible, in both men and women. The doctor should be consulted if the problem is persistent or worrisome.
- *Headache*—this will usually go away after a short time.
- *Nausea*—may occur after a dose, but it will disappear quickly.
- *Nervousness and insomnia (trouble falling asleep or waking often during the night)*—these may occur during the first few weeks; dosage reductions or time will usually resolve them.
- *Agitation (feeling jittery)*—if this happens for the first time after the drug is taken and is more than temporary, the doctor should be notified.

- Any of these side effects may be amplified when an SSRI is combined with other medications that affect serotonin. In most extreme cases, such a combination of medications (e.g., an SSRI and an MAOI) may result in a potentially serious or even fatal "serotonin syndrome," characterized by fever, confusion, muscle rigidity, and cardiac, liver, or kidney problems.

The small number of people for whom MAOIs are the best treatment need to avoid taking decongestants and consuming certain foods that contain high levels of tyramine, such as many cheeses, wines, and pickles. The interaction of tyramine with MAOIs can bring on a sharp increase in blood pressure that can lead to a stroke. The doctor should furnish a complete list of prohibited foods that the individual should carry at all times. Other forms of antidepressants require no food restrictions. MAOIs also should not be combined with other antidepressants, especially SSRIs, due to the risk of serotonin syndrome. . . .

Although not common, some people have experienced withdrawal symptoms when stopping an antidepressant too abruptly. Therefore, when discontinuing an antidepressant, gradual withdrawal is generally advisable.

2

Antidepressants Are an Effective Treatment for Depression

Betty Smartt Carter

Betty Smartt Carter is a writer who lives in Leeds, Alabama. In 1995 she published her first novel, I Read It in the Wordless Book.

Depression causes feelings of sadness and pointlessness that severely inhibit a person's ability to lead a normal life. While it is argued that therapy or natural medicines can help depressed people feel better, antidepressants are the only treatment that truly relieves depression. Antidepressants fix imbalances in the brain's chemistry that lead to feelings of sadness and worthlessness. Although taking antidepressants does not completely erase all feeling of sadness, it does enable depressed people to feel happy when they otherwise could not.

Living in Alabama, I encounter a lot of intuitive spelling. I am no spelling snob. In fact, a roadside sign for "Bowled Peanuts" can brighten my whole day, as can a hand-painted billboard exhorting me to "Give Your Loved One A Missage For Christmas." Never, though, have I taken so much pleasure from a spelling exception as the sign at a local health food store. "WE NOW HAVE ST. JOHN'S WART" proclaimed the movable-type sign out front. I imagined dusty all-terrain vehicles screeching up to the curb, relic collectors jostling to be the first through the door.

Betty Smartt Carter, "Taming the Beast: My Life on Antidepressants," *The Christian Century*, vol. 120, August 9, 2003, p. 21. Copyright © 2003 by The Christian Century Foundation. Reproduced by permission.

The storeowners had intended to advertise St John's Wort, the herbal supplement that many people take to ease depression. It's not clear whether St. John's Wort (hypericum perforatum) actually works. A 2002 study showed that it had no more effect on depressed patients than a sugar pill (*Journal of the American Medical Association*). On the day I drove past that little store, though, hypericum perforatum had just the right effect on me. Yes, I was depressed, but I felt a momentary lift, an escape from the gloom that followed me everywhere: I laughed. If only I could have prolonged that laugh for a few more miles, a few more days.

Feelings of Sadness

People experience sadness in many ways. I know it as a smothering pointlessness. A good laugh felt like taking a big gulp of air—only after that gulp I wanted another, and so I was always finding new things to laugh about. [Light opera composers] Gilbert and Sullivan worked for me. So did [writer] Flannery O'Connor, old Doris Day movies, [writer] Garrison Keillor, and the front page of the tabloid *Weekly World News*. But I laughed at myself more than anything else. I had learned from Woody Allen movies that neuroses can be funny. Weren't my phobias comical? Weren't my compulsive behaviors, my screwy obsessive relationships hilarious?

> *People experience sadness in many ways. I know it as a smothering pointlessness.*

When I finally went to a pastoral counselor, she asked me if I'd sought help before. I told her the funniest thing I could think of—how when my husband and I had once made an appointment for marriage therapy, the counselor suddenly left his wife and ran off with a patient. Telling her about this, I nearly fell off my chair laughing at the irony of it, gulping for air.

She stared at me in the annoying way that was going to become very familiar over the next year. "Why," she asked me, "do you always laugh so hard at sad things?"

That question drew me up short. If somebody asked me the same question now, I'd have a ready reply. I'd say that nobody wants to feel sad, thank you, and that laughter eases sadness in two ways. First, it diminishes a wound by diminishing the situation or person that inflicts the wound—making the victimizer less potent, more easily overcome. Second, research shows that laughter releases serotonin in the brain. So comedy is a natural antidepressant!

At the time, though, I saw myself clearly through the eyes of my therapist—giggling inhumanely at somebody else's tragedy, either because I was too self-absorbed to feel affected or because I was afraid of being sad. The choice before me looked fundamental: did I want to be a cold person laughing or a warm person weeping? Other people have different choices to make, but the question of when to suffer and when to seek relief is there for everybody at some point. It takes many forms, some mundane, others momentous. Should I go for a walk or have another beer? Live without the things I want or sink into debt? Stay in this bad marriage or get a divorce? Even looking to Jesus' example for guidance—choosing love over self-interest—there's much left for us to interpret. Is it more loving, for instance, to bail a rebel son out of jail or leave him there overnight to learn about consequences?

I've noticed that when the choice looks moral or spiritual, we often choose the benefits of suffering—especially for others (Sometimes love must be tough, son! See you in the morning!). When a problem is physical, though, most people opt to relieve the pain. Liberals and conservatives reach for the [pain medication] Loritab with about equal alacrity. Maybe this dual approach to pain makes sense, since there's no obvious benefit from simply enduring bodily illness, no hope of overcoming a bad headache by living through it. Enduring a bad marriage may strengthen the will and teach the heart to overcome, but living with a chronic migraine can wear a body down.

Fixing a Chemical Imbalance

In the case of mental illness, however, the wide range of problems that appear moral/spiritual may actually arise from the physical chemistry of the body. "She really needs a kick in the butt," someone tells you about a mutual friend. "She doesn't do anything all day, just lies around and stares at the wall." While it's possible that the accused is lazy, it's more probable that she's physically sick (depressed), and that relief is only a slight alteration of her brain chemistry away. Many would argue that it's possible for her to feel better without taking drugs: she could try the "talking cure" (regular sessions with a counselor), or an alternative treatment such as herbal or light therapy. If she goes to an M.D. though, she'll likely carry away a prescription for an antidepressant such as Prozac or Zoloft—one of those brave new medicines that promise such good results with so few side effects.

> *For about eight years I've taken fluoxetine (Prozac). Twice I've tried to live without it, only to slide back into gloomy, horizontal wall-staring.*

For about eight years I've taken fluoxetine (Prozac). Twice I've tried to live without it, only to slide back into gloomy, horizontal wall-staring. Lately I've begun to thank God for it, this chemical that—if scientists are right, and they aren't even sure—inhibits my overly efficient reuptake of another chemical (serotonin) that somehow facilitates communication between nerve cells in my brain. I don't understand why I feel so bad when those nerve cells are on the outs: I only know that when they're getting along better, so am I. And so are my husband and children, who don't like to see me sad. For their sake I swallow my pride, and swallow the pill.

Have I sold out to a materialistic view of the universe? Does accepting the importance of the chemicals in my brain preclude a more spiritual view of emotion and thought? It seems to me that the value of consciousness lies in who created it rather than in how it happens. I imagine the neurotransmitters in my brain as, collectively, an instrument of perception, a kind of ear meant to pick up on the purpose of my existence. Fluoxetine is a tiny hearing aid: it amplifies the teleological strain in the material world's great cacophony. Without it, I'm pretty deaf to anything in life that sounds like a point.

Fighting Depression

Yet I do see the pitfalls of trying to overcome emotional pain apart from an accompanying emotional struggle. Whenever I tell my sister that I'm feeling worried, mad, sad or guilty, she says without blinking twice, "Up your dosage." I laugh because it's a running joke between us. I say, "Yeah, and you'd probably give Paxil to Hitler so he wouldn't feel bad about himself." It seems right that I should sometimes feel terrible about things in my life. After all, terrible things happen in my life, often as a result of my own wrong-headedness. I worry that I'll medicate myself so thoroughly that I'll lose my desire to work hard at being a better person.

But I think again of my counselor's question: "Why do you always laugh at sad things?" I was already taking Prozac. She never recommended that I stop taking it or stop laughing. What good would that do? Depression had no particular value of its own. Depression was a thief. It stole my hope and energy and even my affection for my family. It was a beast, and when it had me in its jaws, I'd do about anything to get free. . . .

A Better Life with Antidepressants

The hardest times for me come when the feelings of pointlessness crowd in, as they still do. Then I don't want to see people, much less serve them, laugh with them, weep over them. Verses from Ecclesiastes pop into my brain. All is vanity, say the unconnected nerve endings. I start to see love itself as a lie, just empty cheerfulness spinning its wheels. Love doesn't contain anything, doesn't go anywhere that matters.

But I choose to believe that pointlessness is the lie. I choose to believe that the sane woman—the sane me—is the one with the happy brain neurons, shaking hands and smiling—thanks to the serotonin molecules that float around in there like tiny diplomats, while fluoxetine stands guard at the door.

Yes, that "sane" woman is often sad, often worried or angry—the world is still a pretty tragic place, and no amount of serotonin can change that. But she's also happy a good part of the time. She finds joy in giving herself to people, even though love brings pain. She remembers that there's a reward ahead. And when really dark times come, she prays for help, opens [the inspirational book] *The Habit of Being*, and does her very best impression of Doris Day.

3

Antidepressants Are Not the Most Effective Treatment for Depression

Barry Duncan, Scott Miller,
and Jacqueline Sparks

Barry Duncan is an associate professor at the School of Social and Systemic Studies at Nova Southeastern University in Fort Lauderdale, Florida. Scott Miller is a therapist and an international workshop presenter based in Chicago, Illinois. They are cofounders of the Institute for the Study of Therapeutic Change (ISTC). Jacqueline Sparks is a member of ISTC and a doctoral candidate at Nova Southeastern University.

In Western culture antidepressants have been elevated to the status of miracle drugs, commonly seen as providing a simple solution to the problem of depression. People are bombarded with the idea that a little pill can solve their problems. In reality, antidepressants are not a simple solution and their effectiveness has been exaggerated. Stories of people's miraculous recoveries from depression after taking antidepressants are actually far more rare than the public is led to believe. The strategies that drug companies use to market antidepressants give the public a distorted view of their effectiveness because they fail to mention the medications' side effects and promote the drugs as an easy cure for depression. Moreover, scientific

Barry Duncan, Scott Miller, and Jacqueline Sparks, "Exposing the Mythmakers," *Family Therapy Networker*, vol. 24, March/April 2000, p. 24. Copyright © 2000 by the Institute for the Study of Therapeutic Change. Reproduced by permission.

evidence does not support the claims of the pharmaceutical companies that make antidepressants.

There was a time when therapists, and much of our larger culture, saw depression and other human troubles as complex conditions of mind and heart, influenced by many subtle inner and outer forces. But in the last decade, a vast intellectual and emotional sea change has taken place. We now inhabit a culture where many people hold the view that their emotional pain is "biochemical" and can be cured by simply taking a pill. Emotional suffering, according to this new view, is a genetic glitch, successfully treatable by drugs. Depression is no longer thought to be shaped by such diverse forces as a sedentary, lonely or impoverished life; the loss of love, health or community; "learned helplessness" or feelings of powerlessness arising from unsatisfying work or an abusive relationship. Its resolution no longer requires anyone to get meaningful support from others, to establish a collaborative relationship with a good psychotherapist, to draw on community resources, or for communities to address conditions that breed depression. No, depression is now publicly defined as a purely biological illness, treatable—thank heaven—by the miracle antidepressants.

> *These views [of antidepressants as miracle drugs] have taken on the luster of scientific truths. But they are not truths. They are myths.*

Consider, for example, this interview, which ran on the CBS news program '60 Minutes' in 1991, three years after [the antidepressant] Prozac began its meteoric rise to therapeutic dominance: [CBS interviewer] Lesley Stahl: [voice-over] . . . For 10 years, Maria Romero has been suffering from depression, a serious illness. Sometimes she spends weeks on an unmade bed, in a filthy apartment. She told us that she didn't care about anything, and she often thought of suicide. . . . Most doctors believe chronic depression like Romero's is caused by a chemical imbalance in the brain. To correct it, the doctor prescribed Prozac . . . and two and a half weeks later, we paid her another visit.

Stahl: *"I can't get over it. You're smiling."*

Romero: "Thank you. Yeah."

"How do you feel?"

"Great. I feel great. I feel like—like I'm a different person, somebody else. Somebody—something left my body and another person came in."

"She no longer spends her days in a filthy apartment. So two weeks after you started on this drug, whammo? . . . You stopped being depressed?"

"I stopped being depressed."

"Got out of bed . . . fixed your apartment, fixed yourself, and are losing—"

"—Fixed my life—"

"—weight."

"Yeah. Mmm-hmm. Yep. I'm happy about it. I think it's great."

The Miracle Drug Myth

In the eight years since this segment was broadcast, hundreds of stories like Romero's have been whispered between close friends, described by journalists and repeated in books like Peter Kramer's bestseller, *Listening to Prozac.* They have become our culture's conventional wisdom. The grinding despair and helplessness of depression is, these stories imply, just a "chemical imbalance" somewhat like diabetes or high blood pressure. The treatment of choice, we are told, is always a drug: Prozac, another Selective Serotonin Reuptake Inhibitor (SSRI) like Zoloft or Paxil, or perhaps another, newer antidepressant like Wellbutrin or Serzone. These miraculous drugs, the story goes, are effective with 75 to 85 percent of the people who take them. In this prevailing cultural script, therapy, like an old character actor, is sometimes ignored altogether, and never given more than a minor supporting role. Only one solution, apparently, is needed, and only one is offered: the passive consumption of a pill.

These views have taken on the luster of scientific truths. But they are not truths. They are myths. They have not been confirmed by the latest discoveries of neuroscience, nor are they supported by outcome research.[1] They seem true because they have been repeated and reinforced by mass-market advertising intended to make taking antidepressants seem as normal and pervasive as swallowing aspirin: Zoloft's logo smiles from

---

1. research that looks only at the end result

long-distance calling cards, coffee mugs, luggage tags and complimentary pens and pencils. A commercial during the World Series trumpets Paxil's power to cure social anxiety disorder. And the sides of colorful tissue boxes in physicians' offices proclaim: "Sue's playing with her kids again," "Walter's fishing again" and "Just like normal—thanks to Prozac!" SSRIs, these advertising campaigns imply, are simply the best first choice for treating depression.

> *Not only are side effects underrated and underreported, outcome research does not confirm the miracle status these drugs have been accorded in the popular imagination.*

The message is seductive and it works: if these drugs were books, they would be runaway bestsellers. More than 130 million prescriptions were written for them last year [1999] alone, and more than $8.58 billion was spent on them. And while most mental health professionals would acknowledge that the explanation given to clients is a gross oversimplification of actual brain functioning, few reject the biochemical model altogether. Fewer still question the effectiveness of the drugs. . . .

On a level playing field, antidepressants would be regarded as one valid therapeutic choice among many—one with risks far more grave than those usually attendant on therapy. The awareness of many side effects is just beginning to make it into mainstream consciousness, and the future may reveal further unanticipated consequences: witness the silent epidemics of drug addiction among American women in the 1950s, produced by the widespread prescribing of "mother's little helpers"—amphetamine diet pills and [the tranquilizer] Librium.[2]

Exaggerated Effectiveness

Not only are side effects underrated and underreported, outcome research does not confirm the miracle status these drugs have been accorded in the popular imagination. Our culture's

2. Many women were prescribed these pills to treat anxiety and later became addicted.

exaggerated faith in these psychiatric medications rests not on science, but on brilliant marketing by a profit-driven industry. Outcome research—even outcome research funded by the companies that manufacture pharmaceuticals—has not found these drugs to be any better than therapy, and only marginally better than placebos. Knowing what the research really says will empower therapists to challenge the myths our culture holds about psychoactive medications, reinvigorate their belief in therapy and offer their clients choices based on fact, not superstition masquerading as science.

The first and perhaps most pervasive myth about SSRIs and other newer antidepressants is that their effectiveness is a matter of scientific record, conclusively demonstrated in strict, controlled, double-blind, placebo studies—the gold standard in medical research. According to this myth, the development of SSRIs was a pharmaceutical watershed and the drugs are "magic bullets" far more effective than the older tricyclic antidepressants like Elavil. This message is not only retailed by drug companies, but by the mass media and professional journals: in October 1995, for instance, the American Association for Marriage and Family Therapy's (AAMFT) *Family Therapy News* cited "overwhelming evidence" in support of antidepressants and their undisputed effectiveness with all but 25 percent of people suffering from unipolar depression.

> *Miracle stories . . . are more rare than we have been led to believe.*

This is a gross overstatement. Last year [1999], a federal research review of hundreds of clinical trials found that the newer antidepressants were effective with only half of the depressed people who took them and outperformed placebos by only 18 percent. The finding came from the federal Agency for Health Care Policy and Research (AHCPR), a branch of the Public Health Service that promotes "evidence based" health care practices. . . .

There Is No Miracle Pill

Even at the anecdotal level, miracle stories like Maria Romero's are more rare than we have been led to believe: an online survey of 1,400 depressed people by the National Depressive and Manic Depressive Association (NDMDA) in November 1999 found that 25 percent reported that antidepressants had no effect on their symptoms, 40 percent reported no improvement in fatigue and loss of energy and 35 percent reported no increase in their ability to experience pleasure. . . .

> *In all of the healing arts, there is no single explanation or simple, infallible remedy for any of the problems that beset humankind.*

In all of the healing arts, there is no single explanation or simple, infallible remedy for any of the problems that beset humankind. Yet the growing power of the biological perspective in mental health discourse and practice suggests not only that there are solely biological explanations, but perfect, fail-safe biological solutions as well—simple pills that mark finis[3] to everything from mild depression and nervous tension to panic attacks, bipolar disorder and full-blown psychosis and schizophrenia. How did this scientifically anomalous, weirdly simplistic point of view come about? If the science behind the advertised superiority of psychotropic drugs is so lacking, how did medications come to hold almost unchallenged sway over both public and professional opinion?

In the days of the Watergate investigation,[4] the government informant known as "Deep Throat" met with *Washington Post* reporters Carl Bernstein and Bob Woodward in an underground garage and advised them to "follow the money" if they wanted to find who was really behind the break-in at Democratic National Committee Headquarters. The same advice can help explain why psychiatric medications have permeated every aspect of our culture. Follow the money, and you will begin to understand the growth of the pharmaceutical behemoth.

Drug Companies Distort Public Opinion

In March 1992, *Consumer Reports* estimated that the $63 billion drug industry spent $5 billion a year on promotion and public-

3. the end   4. the political scandals involving former president Richard Nixon between 1972 and 1974

ity, and it spends at least as much today: advertising in medical journals, on television and in women's magazines; helping fund "public awareness" efforts like the National Depression Awareness Day; giving grants to organizations like the Anxiety Disorder Association of America (ADAA), the National Depressive and Manic Depressive Association (NDMDA) and even the American Association for Marriage and Family Therapy (AAMFT). The American Psychiatric Association confirms that at least 30 percent of its budget is now underwritten by drug companies through grants, glossy paid advertisements in its journals and paid exhibits at professional conferences. Psychotherapy organizations cannot begin to compete with this billion-dollar promotional machine, even though the data upholding the value of therapy are clear.

> *Our exaggerated sense of the efficacy of psychiatric drugs may also be colored by the fact that drug companies are under no obligation to publish the results of failed clinical trials.*

Drug companies also fund much of the drug research that supports, however weakly, the myths that have taken hold of almost everyone from psychiatrists and journalists to therapists and the average client in the street. Because of the shrinking of federal grants and the privatization of research funding that began in the [former U.S. president Ronald] Reagan years, pharmaceutical companies now pay for the majority of clinical trials of drugs. The AHCPR metareview, for example, noted that out of 315 published clinical trials of 29 antidepressant drugs, every study that identified a sponsor had been funded by a drug company. The ubiquity of drug company funding may also help account for the dearth of research comparing the effectiveness of therapy and medication: why would drug companies fund research that might prove a competing product (such as therapy) was equally or more effective? . . .

Our exaggerated sense of the efficacy of psychiatric drugs may also be colored by the fact that drug companies are under no obligation to publish the results of failed clinical trials. Thomas J. Moore, a health policy analyst at George Washington University, for example, recently found, in a search of FDA

[Food and Drug Administration] files, the results of two identical trials of the antidepressant Serzone. The one showing a marginally positive result was published, but Moore found no indication that the other trial, showing no measurable drug effect, was ever published. . . .

Adrift in this cultural sea of overprescription and overpromotion, what is the responsible therapist to do? The solution is not to dismiss SSRIs and other antidepressants out of hand, but to put them in their place. Therapists should stop kowtowing to their supposedly superior powers and think of them as one choice among many—and certainly not as the treatment of first resort.

4

The Most Effective Treatment for Depression Is Antidepressants in Combination with Psychotherapy

Tufts University Health and Nutrition Letter

The Tufts University Health and Nutrition Letter *is published by the Gerald J. & Dorothy R. Friedman School of Nutrition Science and Policy at Tufts University, Boston. It aims to provide readers with honest, reliable, and scientifically authoritative health and nutrition advice.*

The overemphasis on medication as the primary treatment for depression has led to large numbers of depressed people being treated solely with antidepressants. Although antidepressants are effective, they are not a cure-all for depression. Another treatment option, psychotherapy, should also be recommended by doctors as an alternative or a complement to antidepressant medication. Therapists teach patients how to establish new patterns of positive thinking that help to prevent future relapses. Antidepressants and psychotherapy are both effective for treating depression and should be used in conjunction to best combat it.

Loss of pleasure, feelings of worthlessness, fatigue, inappropriate guilt, difficulty concentrating, thoughts of suicide. Every year, depression afflicts an estimated 19 million Americans, making it the leading cause of disability in the US. The good news is that more than four out of five people with depression will improve with appropriate treatment. Better news still is that more and more Americans are seeking treatment for depression, in part due to the decreased stigma associated with mental illness and more public awareness about the condition.

An "Over-Emphasis on Medication"

However, as more people get treated, another trend is occurring—they are overwhelmingly being treated with antidepressant medications only. That's at least partly because the front-line treaters of depression tend to be primary care physicians, who are writing prescriptions for antidepressants like Prozac, Paxil, and Zoloft at increasing rates but aren't necessarily recommending psychotherapy as an alternative or complement to medication. Indeed, the proportion of people seeking treatment for depression who were prescribed a drug rose from 45 percent in 1987 to nearly 80 percent in 1997, while the percentage of people receiving psychotherapy for depression during that same 10-year period declined from 71 percent to 60 percent.

> *It's not that antidepressants can't be highly effective—they often are, in fact. But like most drugs, they're not a cure-all.*

In addition to the not uncommon practice by physicians of writing a prescription for an antidepressant after just 15 minutes with a patient, "pressures in managed care settings" are contributing to the "over-emphasis on medication and paucity of psychotherapy," according to Ronald Pies, MD, clinical professor of psychiatry at Tufts University School of Medicine.

Drugs Versus Psychotherapy: It's Not Either/Or

It's not that antidepressants can't be highly effective—they often are, in fact. But like most drugs, they're not a cure-all. "You wouldn't just give people a pill for heart disease or diabetes," says Helen Mayberg, MD, professor of psychiatry and neurology at Emory University [in Atlanta, Georgia]. An equally important part of treating those conditions is addressing people's lifestyle habits, which also play a role in those diseases. It's the same with depression. A reliance solely on pills means that patients miss out on the benefits—the approach to life—psychotherapy can provide.

> *While antidepressants make biochemical changes, therapy helps the brain 'unlearn' depressive thinking.*

Indeed, psychotherapy, when provided expertly, may be as effective as medication. For some people it may be even more effective than drugs. "The current system overmedicates people who might just need therapy," says Dr. Mayberg. For instance, a 2003 study found that psychotherapy was more effective than medication for patients who experienced early childhood trauma. But overall, Dr. Mayberg notes, a combination of antidepressants and psychotherapy appears to be better than either alone (although people who are very apathetic or disengaged may need to start taking an antidepressant before they can fully benefit from psychotherapy).

Earlier this year [2004], Dr. Mayberg and colleagues at the University of Toronto published a study that helps explain why people might benefit more from antidepressants and psychotherapy combined than from either alone. The researchers compared brain scans from people with depression who completed psychotherapy with scans from patients who were treated with the antidepressant paroxetine (Paxil). The researchers discovered that the treatments don't act on the same places in the brain. "They target complementary but nonoverlapping parts," explains Dr. Mayberg. For example, patients who had psychotherapy had brain changes in the cortex, the brain's "thinking structure," while the Paxil appeared to uniquely target structures deep in the brain like the limbic system, the brain's emotion center. The fact that the two types of treatment target different areas suggests to Dr. Mayberg that the effects of medication and therapy are symbiotic. While antidepressants make biochemical changes, therapy helps the brain "unlearn" depressive thinking.

How Psychotherapy Combats Depressive Thoughts

There are several different forms of psychotherapy that have been shown to be effective in treating people with depression, but the form that has been studied most extensively and been found to be particularly beneficial is cognitive therapy. This type of therapy, similar to the type used in Dr. Mayberg's research, teaches patients the connections between their thoughts and their emotions. When depressed, people's thoughts are usually distorted and exaggerated—I'm a failure; I'll never get a job; I'm a terrible mother.

> *Patients who are treated successfully with therapy do quite well a year or two following treatment. That's not true of patients on medication who go off it.*

A cognitive therapist helps set things straight by guiding patients in identifying, evaluating, and ultimately changing distorted thinking. What it comes down to is that "patients are taught by a cognitive therapist to be skeptical when in an extreme emotional state," explains Robert DeRubeis, PhD, professor of psychology at the University of Pennsylvania. Thus, "when they are becoming sad or angry, they think about the thoughts behind their emotions and ask whether they stand up to closer inspection."

Dr. DeRubeis provides this example: When a person catches himself having a negative thought, like "I'm a failure," he can ask himself specific questions, such as what is the evidence that this thought is true? What is the evidence that it is not true? Are there alternative ways to view the situation? Then, he may conclude, "I didn't do as well as I would have liked in this situation, but there were other factors involved. And besides, I have sometimes succeeded in similar situations in the past."

Over the course of therapy, which generally involves 15 to 20 sessions over a 3- to 4-month period, "patients begin to see patterns in their thoughts and learn how to step back to get a more accurate view of themselves," says Dr. DeRubeis. After therapy is completed, people can continue to do these exercises in their head or on paper so that even if they "still have a tendency to attribute blame to themselves, they learn how to catch themselves" before negative thinking consumes them. Cognitive therapists generally provide patients with "refresher" sessions following initial treatment to use on an "as needed" basis, if, say, they need help coping with a stressful change in their life.

Preventing Relapse

The life-long skills learned in cognitive therapy may help explain research showing that patients who complete this kind of treatment successfully are better protected against depression relapse than patients on antidepressants who discontinue them. "Patients who are treated successfully with therapy do quite well a year or two following treatment. That's not true of patients on medication who go off it," says Dr. DeRubeis.

Tufts's Dr. Pies agrees, saying that "there's no demonstrable enduring benefit of medication" once it's discontinued. A person who has a single episode of mild to moderate depression will probably be able to go off antidepressants 6 to 9 months after he or she recovers from the episode, Dr. Pies says, but people who have had multiple depressive episodes usually need to stay on medication indefinitely because their risk of recurrence is so high.

The fact that so many people have to take antidepressants long-term weakens the managed-care argument that medication is cheaper than therapy. Unfortunately, health insurance plans still favor drugs over therapy. Even plans that cover psychotherapy often cover only four or five sessions, not a complete course, although that could change through patient advocacy.

5

Antidepressants Are More Effective than Placebos

Michael Fumento

Michael Fumento is a senior fellow at the Hudson Institute in Washington, D.C., and author of BioEvolution: How Biotechnology Is Changing Our World.

Many researchers falsely claim that antidepressant drugs are no more effective than placebos in treating depression. In reality research has shown that antidepressants are far superior to placebos and that the placebo effect is actually low. Claims that antidepressants do not work are based on flawed drug trials that produce skewed results. For example, researchers frequently exclude patients with severe depression, who are most helped by taking antidepressants, or they conduct short studies that do not allow enough time for antidepressant drugs to begin working. In reality antidepressants are far superior to placebos and better at preventing relapses.

Few drugs inspire more animosity among people who don't use them than Prozac and its antidepressant cousins. On the one hand, they're derisively described as "happy pills," capable of slapping a smiley face on anyone. Actually, decades of research have shown that only those suffering true clinical depression benefit from them. Even then, the pills merely bring patients up to the level of non-depressed persons.

A second, contradictory claim is that the pills don't work at all, except psychosomatically. Every so often a researcher re-leases an analysis of clinical drug trials that purportedly shows that antidepressants are little more effective than placebos. It is little wonder that these analyses always reach the same conclu-sion, because they always use the same methodology and the same data source. These reports are not only as baseless as the "happy pill" attacks; they're downright dangerous because they can encourage depressed people to quit taking their medicine.

The Drug Trials and Distorted Results

The latest such analysis appeared recently in the American Psy-chological Association journal, *Prevention and Treatment* (July 15, 2002). Chiefly authored by University of Connecticut psy-chologist Irving Kirsch, it combined clinical trials of six differ-ent antidepressants. Kirsch's conclusion was that "80 percent of the response to medication was duplicated in placebo control groups." Given the potential side-effects of antidepressants, Kirsch opined, "Medication might best be considered a last re-sort." Several pundits then pumped out op-eds claiming that this same conclusion had been reached in an article by psychi-atrist Arif Khan of the Northwest Clinical Research Center in Bellevue, Washington—notwithstanding that neither the article nor even a promotional press release about it had appeared at the time.

> *[Researcher Irving] Kirsch's analysis [that placebos are as effective as antidepressants] is so filled with problems that it's downright depressing in itself.*

To turn to what *has* been published, however, Kirsch's analysis is so filled with problems that it's downright depress-ing in itself. One Godzilla-sized clue that something is terribly wrong with his conclusion is that the trials he lumped to-gether, when looked at individually, show that the various an-tidepressants themselves are fairly consistent with each other in how well they treat various facets of depression. What changes from study to study is the efficacy of the *placebo*.

How can this be?

The difference between the drug and the placebo is greatly determined by several factors, including the intensity of the depression, the duration of the illness, and even the length of the clinical trial itself.

The Placebo Effect Is Actually Low

"At the milder end of depression, that without mania or mood-swings, you get about a 40 percent response rate [signifying effectiveness] for placebos," notes Steven Dubovsky, professor of psychiatry at the University of Colorado Medical School, Denver. "But if you look at psychotic depression, the response rate is zero. For other severe forms and for chronic depression, the response rate is also very low," he told me. Dr. Khan himself, in a commentary in the February 2002 *Journal of Clinical Pharmacology*, stated this: "The frequency of statistically significant differences between antidepressants and placebos was higher in the trials that included patients with more severe depression," he wrote.

> *The clinical trials also showed antidepressants to be clearly superior in preventing relapses.*

This completely refutes Kirsch's conclusion, because the worst-off patients are generally kept out of clinical trials. "You cannot participate if you're suicidal, because people think it's unethical to give placebos to people who might kill themselves," explains Dr. Dubovsky. "They also usually exclude anybody with concomitant illness, extreme depression, and chronic depression."

Also exaggerating the apparent placebo effect is the fact that the studies define "response rates" as an improvement of at least 50 percent. "But who goes to the doctor for a 50 percent improvement?" asks Dr. Dubovsky. The higher the threshold for defining "improvement," the more effective the antidepressants look.

Antidepressants Are Proven Superior to Placebos

Placebos may also appear in some studies as effective as antidepressants or even more so because the power of the placebo can be immediate, whereas antidepressants take weeks or months to begin working. "The older studies lasted only four weeks," Dr. Dubovsky notes. "Even the newer ones will go only six to eight weeks. Yet there's good recent data showing that some patients may take up to three months to get a full response, especially with severe depression." Short studies don't give the real drugs time to kick in, and they don't allow for the effect of placebos to fade away. Yet Kirsch's analysis and others that have reached similar conclusions lump all the outcomes together, regardless of study length.

The clinical trials also showed antidepressants to be clearly superior in preventing relapses. According to Dr. Walter Brown, clinical professor of psychiatry at Brown University Medical School in Providence, Rhode Island, "Among patients who have improved with an antidepressant and are then assigned to either placebo or drug continuation, it is not uncommon for those assigned to drug to have a relapse rate of about 10 percent over a year but those assigned to placebo to have close to a 50 percent relapse."

Finally, the duration of the depression doesn't influence the response to antidepressants, but it does to placebos. "Placebo response rates as low as 13 percent have been reported in patients depressed for two years or more, with drug response rates in the same patients close to 60 percent," according to Brown.

With antidepressant drug trials, insufficient attention to these details makes for lousy science. When the subject is a debilitating and costly disease that often ends in suicide, it can be the scientific equivalent of involuntary manslaughter.

6

Antidepressants Are Not Significantly More Effective than Placebos

Irving Kirsch and David Antonuccio

Irving Kirsch is professor of psychology at the University of Connecticut. David Antonuccio is professor of psychiatry and behavioral sciences at the University of Nevada School of Medicine and director staff psychologist for the stop smoking program at the Reno Veterans Affairs Medical Center.

Antidepressants are considered by many people to be highly effective for treating depression; however, research shows that they are not significantly better than placebos. In clinical trials depressed patients did benefit from antidepressant medication, but placebo treatments were only slightly less effective than antidepressants. Although antidepressants may help some people, the difference in the effectiveness of the drug and placebos is not enough to justify the widespread use of antidepressants to treat depression. Antidepressants should only be used as a last resort for treating depression.

Antidepressants are widely believed to be exceptionally effective medications. The data, however, tell a different story. [In 2002, researchers Irving Kirsch, Thomas J. Moore, Alan Scoboria, and Sarah S. Nicholls] analyzed the data sent to the U.S. Food and Drug Administration [FDA] by the manufacturers of the six most widely prescribed antidepressants (fluoxetine [Prozac], paroxetine [Paxil], sertraline [Zoloft], venlafaxine [Ef-

Irving Kirsch and David Antonuccio, "Antidepressants Versus Placebos: Meaningful Advantages Are Lacking," *Psychiatric Times*, vol. xix, September 2002. Copyright © 2002 by CMP Media LLC, 2801 McGaw Ave., Irvine, CA 92614, USA. Reproduced by permission.

fexor], nefazodone [Serzone] and citalopram [Celexa]). Their research showed that although the response to antidepressants was substantial, the response to inert placebo was almost as great. The mean difference was about two points on the Hamilton Rating Scale for Depression (HAM-D).[1] Although statistically significant, this difference is not clinically significant. More than half of the clinical trials sponsored by the pharmaceutical companies failed to find significant drug/placebo difference, and there were no advantages to higher doses of antidepressants. The small difference between antidepressant and placebo has been referred to as a "dirty little secret" by clinical trial researchers, a secret that was believed by FDA officials to be "of no practical value to either the patient or prescriber."

A Small Difference Between Drug and Placebo

Previous reports of vanishingly small drug/placebo differences were met with skepticism. In contrast, the basic findings from this new meta-analysis have been accepted as accurate. The dispute is no longer about the small size of the average drug/ placebo difference, but rather about how to interpret this fact and what to do about it.

> *Research showed that although the response to antidepressants was substantial, the response to inert placebo was almost as great.*

Various interpretive possibilities have been raised. One of the most popular theories is that there may be a subset of patients for whom at least some antidepressants are very effective, but that their relative lack of efficacy with other patients masks effect. Specifically, whereas mildly depressed patients respond to both drugs and placebos, more severely depressed patients respond only to active drugs. The FDA data contradict this hypothesis. Although severely depressed patients benefited more from medication than mildly depressed patients due to a phenomenon known as regression toward the mean, they also

1. a scale used to rate the severity of depression in patients already diagnosed as depressed

benefited more from placebo than their more mildly depressed counterparts. . . .

The Importance of the Difference Between Drug and Placebo

Another popular hypothesis is that drug effects are more stable than placebo effects, resulting in lower relapse rates. This hypothesis is also contradicted by the data. A meta-analysis of relapse prevention trials published between 1973 and 1990 indicated that 71% of the drug response was duplicated by placebo. Kirsch et al.'s meta-analysis also examined response to treatment as a function of the duration of the trial. The data indicated that responses to both drug and placebo decrease over time. Contrary to conventional wisdom, however, the correlation between duration of the trial and response to treatment was higher for active medication than for placebo, suggesting a steeper decline in effectiveness for active drugs than for placebo.

Alternative Solutions as the First Approach

In light of these data, what should be done in clinical contexts? Some have suggested that antidepressants continue to be prescribed, even if their effects are largely placebo effects. If nothing else, these agents can be used as active placebos. Given the side effects of these medications, we suggest an alternative approach. There are many interventions that seem to be as effective or nearly as effective as antidepressants. These include physical exercise, bibliotherapy and psychotherapy. Psychotherapy has the further advantage of demonstrated superiority to medications in long-term comparative studies. Given these data, antidepressant medication might best be considered a last resort, restricted to patients who refuse or fail to respond to other treatments.

7

Antidepressants Help People Even If They Are No More Effective than Placebos

Jacob Sullum

Jacob Sullum is a senior editor for Reason, *a monthly magazine that provides analysis of politics, culture, and ideas.*

Millions of Americans have benefited from using antidepressants to help relieve depression and a wide range of other problems such as panic and anxiety. However, a recent study suggests that people may only feel better while taking these drugs because they expect to. Researchers who studied the effects of both antidepressants and placebos found that there is only a very small difference between the effectiveness of the drug and the placebo. These findings, however, do not change the fact that antidepressants help people feel better. For this reason, many experts believe that antidepressants are still an effective treatment for depression.

I s it possible that everyone who's been listening to Prozac has been hearing things?

During the last decade or so [since 1990], millions of Americans have taken Prozac and similar antidepressants, known as selective serotonin reuptake inhibitors (SSRIs), to help achieve happier, less anxious lives. But a new study suggests that people feel better after taking these drugs mainly because that's what they expect.

Antidepressants Are the Solution

The finding will dismay many people who are convinced that an SSRI was the key to their self-improvement. Just as Viagra, originally approved for treatment of impotence, is now taken as an all-purpose sex enhancer, SSRI use has expanded beyond severe depression to include a wide range of dissatisfactions and problems in living.

In his book *Creating Mental Illness*, the sociologist Allan V. Horwitz observes that so-called antidepressants "work equally well for a broad range of disorders including panic, obsessive, and phobic conditions, as well as depressive and anxious states. They are also widely used for substance abuse and eating disorders and for general distress among both adults and children."

> *A new study suggests that people feel better after taking [antidepressants] mainly because that's what they expect.*

Not only that, but "these medications are promoted as ways to enhance the personalities of *normal* people by improving self-esteem, self-confidence, interpersonal relationships, and achievement." This sort of use was chronicled, somewhat ambivalently, by the psychiatrist Peter D. Kramer in his 1993 bestseller *Listening to Prozac*.

The broad range of applications for which SSRIs are recommended has contributed to the perception that they are too good to be true. A study in the current [July 2002] issue of the American Psychological Association's journal *Prevention and Treatment* lends substantial support to that view.

The Placebo Effect

A team led by University of Connecticut psychologist Irving Kirsch analyzed clinical trial data for six widely prescribed antidepressants approved by the Food and Drug Administration [FDA] between 1987 and 1999: Prozac, Paxil, Zoloft, Effexor, Serzone, and Celexa. They found that "80% of the response to medication was duplicated in placebo control groups."

In other words, subjects who received only the placebo improved almost as much as subjects who got the drug. The average difference in improvement was only two points on the Hamilton Depression Scale,[1] which generates scores up to 50 or 62 points, depending on the version used.

The difference was so small, Kirsch and his colleagues report, that it could be due entirely to patients who surmised, based on side effects, that they were receiving the real drug and therefore had stronger expectations of improvement. If so, the much-ballyhooed SSRIs would be nothing more than placebos themselves. Hence the title of the study: "The Emperor's New Drugs."

"Our data suggest that the effects of antidepressant drugs are very small and of questionable clinical significance," Kirsch et al. conclude. Given the potential side effects of SSRIs, they say, "antidepressant medication might best be considered a last resort, restricted to patients who refuse or fail to respond to other treatments."

The Significance of the Findings

The study is accompanied by nine commentaries. None of them questions Kirsch et al.'s main finding, which is consistent with the results of earlier analyses. But some of the commentators argue that antidepressants may be more beneficial than the FDA data indicate.

"Are these widely touted, intensively marketed drugs as pathetically ineffective as these . . . data suggest?" asks Brown University psychiatrist Walter A. Brown. Perhaps not, he says, if SSRIs are especially helpful to certain kinds of people, such as the severely depressed, or if their effects last longer than the effects of placebos.

"Medication treatment is no less potent than other clinical alternatives," write three psychologists and a psychiatrist. "Psychological mechanisms may account for the bulk of its effects (on average), but it is at the least a very effective way of mobilizing those mechanisms."

Similarly, Daniel E. Moerman, a professor of behavioral sciences at the University of Michigan, says "a doctor with a drug

1. used to rate the severity of depression in patients already diagnosed as depressed

(especially a hot, new one) can be a powerful 'meaning delivery system.'. . . If physicians prescribed placebos alone, their effect would be significantly reduced because doctors have little confidence in them."

The same thing could happen, of course, if physicians and their patients take to heart the evidence indicating that the pharmacological effects of SSRIs are negligible. Calling attention to the placebo effect may be a good way to ruin it.

But perhaps the evidence won't matter. As Moerman observes, "Far too many people experience substantial benefits from these drugs (and/or from the context of their use) to simply let them go."

8

Antidepressants Benefit Children

Sherri Walton and David Fassler

Sherri Walton is an advocate for the use of antidepressants by children. David Fassler is a child and adolescent psychiatrist and a clinical associate professor of psychiatry at the University of Vermont.

Depression is a serious problem among youths. Depression negatively impacts youths' lives by negatively affecting self-esteem, interrupting normal emotional development, interfering with learning, and damaging friendships with peers. This mental disorder also results in over 500,000 adolescent suicide attempts each year. Fortunately, antidepressants can be quite effective in treating children with depression, often saving their lives. However, antidepressants work best when used in conjunction with therapy.

I

My name is Sherri Walton and I am here [in Bethesda, Maryland] as a volunteer advocate. This is my 14-year-old daughter, Jordan. We have traveled here from Arizona at our own expense because we know that public forums, such as this [Food and Drug Administration hearing on antidepressants], usually only hear from those who have had negative experiences. We felt it was important for us to share our story.

Part I: Sherri Walton, testimony before the U.S. Food and Drug Administration Psychopharmacologic Drugs Advisory Committee and the Pediatric Subcommittee of the Anti-Infective Drugs Advisory Committee, Bethesda, Maryland, February 2, 2004. Part II: David Fassler, testimony before the U.S. Senate Committee on Health, Education, Labor, and Pensions, March 1, 2005.

Jordan was diagnosed with Tourette's syndrome[1] when she was 7 year old. As is typical of Tourette's syndrome, she also has OCD [obsessive-compulsive disorder][2] and ADHD [attention-deficit/hyperactivity disorder].[3] She was originally prescribed an [antidepressant] SSRI [selective serotonin reuptake inhibitor] medication to relieve the anxiety that consumed her because she could not control her thoughts or behaviors.

> **❝** *[Antidepressant] medication allowed [my daughter] to participate in, and understand, the cognitive behavior therapy that gave her some semblance of normalcy.* **❞**

This medication allowed her to participate in, and understand, the cognitive behavior therapy that gave her some semblance of normalcy. In fourth grade, Jordan was still being hampered by the obsessive thoughts caused by her OCD. In the classroom, this was overwhelming and extremely frightening for her.

Her medication was changed to a different SSRI and within a few months, her obsessive thoughts became less and less intense. They were still there, but now she was able to recognize what they were and usually work through them.

Dance is Jordan's passion. It is what she wants to do with her life. In November of 2002, she announced she wanted to quit dance. As she burst into tears, she said that she wanted to die, she wanted to kill herself.

She was diagnosed with clinical depression and her medication was changed from the SSRI she had taken for four years to a different SSRI to treat both her OCD and depression.

As Jordan has struggled to find success in school and in her relationships with peers, her meds were sometimes the only thing she could count on to help her. The daughter I have here now standing next to me is a happy, healthy, successful teenager. There is no doubt in my mind that the SSRI medication saved her life, and like the other SSRI antidepressants she is tak-

---

1. a disorder characterized by involuntary repetitive behaviors   2. an anxiety disorder characterized by obsessions and compulsions   3. a disorder characterized by behaviors such as inattentiveness, impulsiveness, and hyperactivity

ing gave her a chance for a full and complete life.

With the greatest sympathy for any families who have lost children to suicide, I ask that you identify and fix any breakdown in the system that could lead to such tragedy. At the same time, I ask that you appreciate and take into account the enormous benefits that these medications have had for children and their families.

II

Mental and behavioral disorders affect an estimated 20 percent of children and adolescents, or approximately 10 million young people. Tragically, only one in five receive any form of treatment for these disorders.

Within this total, clinical depression is a frequently occurring disorder. It is estimated that depression affects 2.5% of children and over 8% of U.S. adolescents. These rates account for approximately 2.6 million youth ages 6–17.

Depression and related mood disorders are serious illnesses for most children and adolescents diagnosed with the condition. Depression can interrupt a youth's normal emotional development, negatively affect self-esteem, interfere with learning in school, and undermine friendships with peers. Over 500,000 adolescents attempt suicide each year and depression is most often the cause.

> *Antidepressants can be helpful and even lifesaving for some children who have complex psychiatric disorders such as depression.*

No single cause of depression has been identified. However, we know that depression is an illness with a pronounced biological basis. Research has clearly demonstrated that depression is associated with deficiencies in specific brain chemicals such as serotonin and norepinephrine. The genes that a child inherits also predispose a person to the illness, but this predisposition, or vulnerability, to depression typically is "triggered" by life events. Researchers have begun to identify these triggers, called risk factors, for depression.

A child's risk for becoming depressed may increase with

stress or with an experience of devastating loss or trauma. Behavioral problems and other psychiatric disorders—for example, conduct, attention-deficit, learning, anxiety, and substance abuse disorders—frequently co-occur with depression and may help explain its onset. A family history of depression or bipolar disorder is also a significant risk factor for depression in a child or young adult.

Because of the severity of the disorder, the AACAP [American Academy of Child and Adolescent Psychiatry] and the APA [American Psychiatric Association] support treatments that have been shown to be effective in reducing the symptoms of depression and promoting normal development.

Antidepressants Are Effective

Medication, specifically antidepressants, can be helpful and even lifesaving for some children who have complex psychiatric disorders such as depression. Medication is most effective when it is used as part of a comprehensive treatment plan, individualized to the needs of the child and family. All children and adolescents who are taking antidepressant medication should be monitored closely by a physician, especially early in the course of treatment, or when medications are being changed or dosages adjusted.

Findings from the NIMH [National Institute of Mental Health]-supported Treatment of Adolescents with Depression Study (TADS) show that a combination of medication and therapy, specifically, Cognitive Behavioral Therapy, or CBT, are more effective than either option used alone. Family therapy and/or work with the child's school may also be appropriate components of a treatment plan. All interventions have potential risks and benefits, and parents need and deserve access to as much information as possible in order to make fully informed decisions regarding treatment options.

It is important to remember that the majority of children and adolescents with depression who are not identified and treated are likely to have ongoing problems in school, at home and with their friends. Research indicates that more than half will eventually attempt suicide, and an estimated 2% to 5% will ultimately die as a result.

9

Antidepressants Have Not Been Proven to Benefit Children

Jon N. Jureidini et al.

Jon N. Jureidini is the head of the Department of Psychological Medicine at the Women's and Children's Hospital in North Adelaide, Australia; Christopher J. Doecke is an associate professor at the University of South Australia; Peter R. Mansfield is a research fellow, and Michelle M. Haby is a senior epidemiologist, at the University of Adelaide, Australia; David B. Menkes is a professor of psychological medicine at the Public Health Department of Human Services in Melbourne, Australia; and Anne L. Tonkin is an associate professor at the University of Wales Academic Unit, Australia.

Antidepressants are increasingly being used as a first-line treatment for depression in children and adolescents. However, a review of studies on these drugs found that in many cases they were only slightly more effective than placebos for treating depressed youth and that they had many serious side effects. Biased and inaccurate reporting of these drug trials has led many doctors and patients to draw overconfident conclusions about the effectiveness and safety of antidepressants. Many reports exaggerate the benefits of antidepressants and ignore or downplay the harm these drugs can cause.

Antidepressants introduced since 1990, especially selective serotonin reuptake inhibitors [SSRIs] and venlafaxine, have

Jon N. Jureidini, Christopher J. Doecke, Peter R. Mansfield, Michelle M. Haby, David B. Menkes, and Anne L. Tonkin, "Efficacy and Safety of Antidepressants for Children and Adolescents," *British Medical Journal*, vol. 328, April 10, 2004, pp. 879–83. Copyright © 2004 by the British Medical Association. Reproduced by permission.

been used increasingly as first line treatment for depression in children. The safety of prescribing antidepressants to children (including adolescents) has been the subject of increasing concern in the community and the medical profession, leading to recommendations against their use from government and industry. In this paper, we review the published literature on the efficacy and safety of newer antidepressants in children. . . .

The Quality of the Drug Trials

Of seven published randomized controlled trials of newer antidepressants for depressed children published in referred journals, six used a placebo control. We analysed each study's methods and the extent to which authors' conclusions were supported by data. . . .

Pharmaceutical companies paid for the trials and otherwise remunerated the authors of at least three of the four larger studies. . . .

Effectiveness of the Drug

A total of 477 patients in the six studies were treated with paroxetine, fluoxetine, sertraline, or venlafaxine, and 464 were treated with placebo. Of 42 reported measures, only 14 showed a statistical advantage for an antidepressant. None of the 10 measures relying on patient reported or parent reported outcomes showed significant advantage for an antidepressant, so that claims for effectiveness were based entirely on ratings by doctors. No study presented data on rates of attempted self harm, presentations to emergency or mental health services, or school attendance.

> *Adverse effects might be more frequent than the authors of these studies imply.*

Two small studies found no statistically significant advantage for antidepressants over placebo on any of the outcome measures reported. Of the remaining four papers, two did and two did not show statistically significant advantages for antidepressants over placebo on primary outcome measures. . . .

Adverse Effects of Treatment

Because of the follow up period for the randomized controlled trials was short, and numbers were relatively small, serious adverse effects were likely to be few. When they do occur, we would therefore expect authors to draw attention to them, along with data available from other sources that suggest that serious adverse effects might occur. Of 93 patients treated with paroxetine [in one study], 11 had serious adverse events, compared with 2/87 in the placebo group. The authors presented no statistical analysis, but the difference was significant. In spite of this striking difference in serious events between paroxetine and placebo, [the researchers M.B. Keller et al.] concluded that, "paroxetine was generally well tolerated in this adolescent population, and most adverse effects were not serious," even though seven patients were admitted to hospital during treatment with paroxetine. Furthermore, despite five of these patients being admitted to hospital with events known to occur with the use of selective serotonin reuptake inhibitors, including suicidality, only one serious event (headache) was judged by the treating investigator to be related to paroxetine treatment. The criteria for determining causation of serious events were not stated.

> *The authors of all of the four larger studies have exaggerated the benefits, downplayed the harms, or both.*

Among 373 patients in [another trial] 9% (17/189) treated with sertraline withdrew because of adverse effects, compared with 3% (5/184) in the placebo group. These authors also published no statistical analysis of this outcome or details of the adverse effects, but the difference in withdrawal rates was significant. [The researchers, K.D. Wagner et al.] reported seven adverse effects that occurred in at least 5% of the sertraline group, at least twice as often as in the placebo. Despite these results they concluded that, "sertraline is an effective, safe, and well tolerated short-term treatment for children and adolescents."

Other sources of data support the view that adverse effects might be more frequent than the authors of these studies imply. For example, children and adolescents with obsessive compulsive disorder exhibit a variety of treatment emergent effects of fluoxetine, including an "activation syndrome" affecting up to half of young patients; self injurious ideation or behaviour was seen in 6/42 patients. The failure of drug companies to disclose increased suicidal activity secondary to these drugs is also the subject of much debate. . . .

Exaggerated Efficacy

Given the large placebo effect in all six studies reviewed, the clinical significance of the drug effect should be questioned. For example, . . . [a 2002 study by researchers G.J. Emslie et al.] found that, for the measure showing the greatest advantage of fluoxetine over placebo . . . the improvement in the placebo group was 70% of the improvement seen in the fluoxetine group. . . . Similarly, the fact that 87% of the improvement in the sertraline group was reproduced in the placebo group casts some doubt on [a 2003 study by Wagner]. . . .

Quality of Reporting

In discussing their own data, the authors of all of the four larger studies have exaggerated the benefits, downplayed the harms, or both. This raises the question of whether the journals that published the research reviewed the studies with a sufficient degree of scrutiny, given the importance of the subject. . . .

Inaccurate Reporting

The trial consistently found large improvements in placebo groups, with statistically significant additional benefits for active drug on some measures only. These results make a major benefit from newer antidepressants unlikely, but a small benefit remains possible. Randomised controlled trials usually underestimate the serious adverse effects of drugs. The fact that serious adverse effects with newer antidepressants are common enough to be detected in randomised controlled trials raises serious concerns about their potential for harm. The magnitude of benefit is unlikely to be sufficient to justify risking those harms, so confidently recommending these drugs as a treatment option, let alone as first line treatment, would be inappropriate.

We are concerned that biased reporting and overconfident recommendations in treatment guidelines may mislead doctors, patients, and families. Many will undervalue non-drug treatments that are probably both safer and more effective. Accurate trial reports are a foundation of good medical care. It is vital that authors, reviewers, and editors ensure that published interpretations of data are more reasonable and balanced than is the case in the industry dominated literature on childhood antidepressants. This is particularly true in the light of the increasing reliance on online abstracts by doctors who lack the time or the skills for detailed analysis of complete trial reports.

10

Antidepressants Increase the Risk of Suicide Among Youths

Susan Schindehette

Susan Schindehette is a senior writer for People Weekly *magazine. Before coming to* People *in 1988, Schindehette was a general assignment reporter in* Time *magazine's Washington bureau.*

Although antidepressants help some children, they can also cause adverse reactions in others. Children may become more agitated, aggressive, and withdrawn when they begin to take antidepressants, increasing the risk of suicidal behavior. More research needs to be conducted on how these drugs affect youths, and they need to be prescribed more judiciously. The experience of Tom and Kathy Woodward illustrates how dangerous it is for parents to be unaware that such serious side effects are possible. The Woodwards believe their daughter Julie, age sixteen, committed suicide because of the adverse effects of the antidepressant Zoloft.

From the very beginning, Tom and Kathy Woodward's first-born was a golden child. At 5 months, she spoke her first word. While still in preschool, she was signed by the Wilhelmina [modeling] agency as a child model. And by the time Julie Woodward reached her sophomore year at a Catholic high school near her home in North Wales, Pa., she was a good student looking forward to a bright future that would include, as she once wrote on a piece of paper titled "Plan for Life," marriage (anytime "over 26"), children ("two or three") and "a nice house in the country."

> *[There is] growing concern that the very drugs meant to lift kids out of depression sometimes do just the opposite.*

Instead, at 16, Julie's life took a dark turn. In the fall of 2002 she began having trouble at a new school and, in defiance of her parents' wishes, began dating a college boy. Julie became quiet and withdrawn, so much so that in July [2003] Tom and Kathy took her to a psychiatrist, who prescribed two antidepressants. She lasted on the medication just one week: On July 23, after discovering that their daughter wasn't home—and hadn't spent the night with her grandparents, as they had thought—her parents became alarmed. Tom walked out to the garage behind the house, opened the door and found Julie, 17, dead. "She had hanged herself," he says, his voice breaking. "I grabbed her, and I knew she was gone. I felt her, and she was cold."

Increasing Numbers of Anguished Parents

Today [April 2004], eight months after the tragedy, the Woodwards still sound as if they are trying to convince themselves that all of this really happened. "Julie was the most self-protective, self-preserving kid in the world," says her mother, Kathy, 47. Adds Tom, 46, who, like his wife, is a financial consultant: "I never in a million years thought this could happen to us."

But it did, and the Woodwards aren't the only parents to suffer such a loss. On March 22 [2004] the FDA [Food and Drug Administration] issued a recommendation for manufacturers to begin printing warning labels for antidepressants, in response to growing concern that the very drugs meant to lift kids out of depression sometimes do just the opposite. "The labeling we are proposing won't say you can't use these drugs," says Dr. Thomas Laughren of the FDA psychiatric drugs division. "[But] the one thing that was clear from our hearings is that many patients were not being well monitored." The labels will caution patients to watch for signs of hostility and agitation, especially during the first days of use and whenever dosage is adjusted.

Exact figures on the number of children on antidepressants who have killed themselves are impossible to come by. In February [2004], 31 families—including the Woodwards—traveled to Washington, D.C., to testify before an FDA panel. There, anguished parents told of sons and daughters who became agitated, aggressive and, in the most extreme cases, suicidal, sometimes within days of the drugs' being prescribed. In addition to warning labels, the agency has ordered further scrutiny of the drugs, many of them SSRIs (for selective serotonin reuptake inhibitors), which, in rare circumstances, have also been suspected as a factor in adult suicide. "We want to make sure if there is the slightest indication these drugs cause suicide that children not be exposed to that," says U.S. Rep. Jim Greenwood (R-Pa.), who has called on drug companies to release unpublished research on the subject. "Right now we are trying to fit the pieces together and sort this thing out."

Limited Testing

It may come as a surprise to parents just how little testing has been done on kids and antidepressants to date. About 1 million children are now taking the drugs, sold under names like Prozac, Celexa and Paxil, and the majority report side effects no more serious than dry mouth and sleeplessness. The benefits, meanwhile, when used in conjunction with other therapy, can be huge. Paradise Valley, Ariz., mother Sherri Walton, 45, describes antidepressants as a lifeline for her 15-year-old daughter Jordan, who has battled Tourette's syndrome, depression and obsessive-compulsive disorder. "Now I have a happy, healthy teenage child who's successful in school and can't wait to get her learner's permit," says Walton. "Her medication helped every step of the way."

> *It may come as a surprise to parents just how little testing has been done on kids and antidepressants to date.*

Yet some doctors complain that information is scarce when it comes to kids and antidepressants. In all, just 4,000 children have taken part in clinical trials for antidepressants. Only one of the drugs, Prozac, carries official FDA approval for treating kids with depression. (Because of the complex way medicines are introduced to the market, other antidepressants that have proven safe and effective in adults may be legally prescribed "off-label."[1]) "[At this point], we're not sure how children and adults react differently," says Dr. Philip Walson, director of clinical trials and pharmacology at Cincinnati Children's Hospital Medical Center. "We need to test these drugs and monitor them and realize that children aren't just little adults." For its part, Pfizer, the company that manufactures [the antidepressant] Zoloft, declines to comment specifically on the Woodward case, although a vice president, Dr. Catherine Clary, says that it will work closely with the FDA to devise label changes for the drug.

Signs of Depression

Caution comes too late for the Woodwards, whose three-story stone house in the Philadelphia suburbs is the kind built for a large family. "You live for your children," says Tom, who coaches track while Kathy teaches Sunday school. Julie, an older sister to Caroline, 16, and brothers Tom, 12, and Brian, 8, was always precocious and introspective. "She was more the observer," says Kathy. As a toddler, "she wanted to go to the park and just see the other kids. She didn't want to be part of the crowd."

> *We need to test these drugs and monitor them and realize that children aren't just little adults.*

But Julie was no loner. At Gwynedd Mercy Academy, her private high school, she played sports and sang in the choir. "Her friends here would say she was a very creative person, a good writer and a good friend," says the school's principal, Sister Kathleen Boyce. But for her junior year, Woodward decided to transfer to a much larger public school. "She wanted the real high school experience," says Kathy. The transition was tough.

1. Off-label use is the prescribing of a medication in a different dose, for a longer duration of time or for a different medical condition than recommended by the FDA.

Julie's grades suffered, and she abandoned old friends and activities. She also began secretly dating the 19-year-old brother of one of her friends. The relationship ended, but not before Julie had stayed out all night and been involved in a minor car accident the next day. "Julie was very depressed," says Lindsay Harris, 17, who had known her since fourth grade. "If you talked about school, she didn't want to talk about it. If you talked about the future, she didn't want to talk about it."

> *If it hadn't been for that drug . . . Julie would still be here with us.*

Kathy Woodward was the first to bring up the idea of counseling for her daughter. "I drove her to the doctor, but she wouldn't get out of the car," says Kathy. The Woodwards eventually had Julie examined by two doctors before a third diagnosed her with depression. Julie enrolled in a group-therapy program at the Horsham Clinic in Ambler, Pa., where the admitting doctor prescribed Zoloft and trazodone, the generic name for another antidepressant often used on patients who are having trouble sleeping. Kathy says she was initially opposed to medicating Julie but, told it was an important part of her therapy, deferred to mental health professionals.

Mood Changes

Julie took her first Zoloft last July 16 [2003] and, six days later, after complaining of insomnia, began taking trazodone. Her moods were mixed: Some days she seemed sweet and contented. On another she argued with Kathy and shoved her to the floor. "I got up and hugged her and said, 'What's that?'" recalls Kathy. "She just kind of looked surprised. It took a few seconds, but she hugged me back."

In the days that followed, Julie celebrated her younger brother's birthday with the family and helped pack for vacation. On the night she died, Kathy left the house to take her three younger kids to softball and a swim meet. Tom was already driving home from work at the time. Out of the blue, Julie called him from home and said that Kathy wanted him to come directly to the swim meet. "I told her I loved her," says Tom, barely able to collect himself. "She told me she loved me too."

The Woodwards weren't terribly concerned that Julie wasn't at home when they returned that night, since she routinely spent nights at her grandparents' house nearby. But the next day, a counselor from the Horsham clinic called to say Julie had missed a therapy session. Now worried, Kathy said she wasn't sure exactly where her daughter was, to which the therapist replied, "You have to find her. Julie had a terrible session on Monday," recalls Kathy. It was later that day that Tom found Julie's body in the garage.

In the wake of her death, police confiscated the teen's computer and journals, and found no mention of suicide. But the family did discover what Tom describes as a "goodbye note" in a backpack that Julie had left at her grandparents' house days earlier. "The whole thing was shocking," says her friend Jacqueline Cellucci, 17. After a period of depression, Julie "seemed much happier. I thought she was fine."

In retrospect, the Woodwards say there may have been signs that Julie was having an adverse reaction to the drug. Her sister Caroline, who shared a room with Julie, now says that Julie, lying in bed, said she was experiencing the feeling of being lifted up toward the ceiling. Other family members recall seeing Julie pacing back and forth in her bedroom several days before the suicide, and rocking back and forth—both possible signs of a condition called akathisia, which can include agitation. (Akathisia has been reported as one of Zoloft's adverse reactions.) An autopsy determined that Julie had a higher-than-expected level of the antidepressant in her blood, which may indicate she was not absorbing the drug as quickly as other patients.

Serious Risks

As in other cases of adolescent suicide, impulsivity may have also been a factor. According to Dr. Norman Fost, a University of Wisconsin pediatrician and bioethicist, antidepressants can create what's called an "activation syndrome" in depressed children—giving them the energy to act on suicidal thoughts. "I don't think these drugs should be prohibited," says Fost, "but anyone prescribing them to adolescents needs to tell parents about the risks."

That is now the Woodwards' fervent hope. Since Julie's death, they've torn down the old wooden garage where she ended her life. But there are other things they cannot bring themselves to do—closing out her checking account or choosing a headstone for her grave, which they often visit. Grappling with questions that may always remain unanswered, they insist there's at least one thing they're certain of. "If it hadn't been for that drug," says her father, "Julie would still be here with us."

11

Antidepressants Do Not Increase the Risk of Suicide Among Youths

Suzanne Vogel-Scibilia

Suzanne Vogel-Scibilia is a psychiatrist and a member of the board of directors of the National Alliance for the Mentally Ill.

No studies have proven that serotonin reuptake inhibitors (SSRIs) cause an increase in suicidal behavior in youths. In fact, such psychotropic medications can significantly improve the outcomes of young people suffering from mental illnesses such as depression. Mentally ill youths treated with medications do better in school, make and keep friends more easily, and are less likely to end up in jails or prisons.

G ood Morning. NAMI (the National Alliance for the Mentally Ill) greatly appreciates this opportunity to provide a statement on the critically important issue of the use of selective serotonin reuptake inhibitors (SSRIs) for children and adolescents with depression—specifically focused on reports of suicidality (ideation and attempts) in clinical trials and approaches to analyzing data from these trials and further research needs to address these issues.

NAMI was founded as a grassroots family advocacy movement 25 years ago in Madison, Wisconsin. Today, NAMI has more than 220,000 consumer and family members nationwide

Suzanne Vogel-Scibilia, testimony before the U.S. Food and Drug Administration Psychopharmacologic Drugs Advisory Committee and the Pediatric Subcommittee of the Anti-Infective Drugs Advisory Committee, Bethesda, Maryland, February 2, 2004.

dedicated to improving the lives of children and adults living with mental illnesses.

My name is Suzanne Vogel-Scibilia and I am a member of the NAMI Board of Directors. As a person diagnosed with bipolar disorder, I am proud to serve on the NAMI Board and proud that NAMI is the nation's "voice on mental illness" representing both consumers and family members. I am also proud to be the mother of five children, two of who are diagnosed with mental illnesses and one of who is currently being treated with an SSRI.

I am also a psychiatrist with board certification in general psychiatry, addiction psychiatry and geriatric psychiatry and have additional board certification from the American Board of Adolescent Psychiatry. I have a thriving practice in Beaver, Pennsylvania.

My son, Anthony, has had severe mental illness, primarily depression and attention deficit disorder, as a manifestation of his bipolar disorder and another son has had treatment with numerous antidepressant medications including several SSRIs. My children have had tremendous improvement with their illnesses and lead very full and functional lives because of SSRI medication, along with other psychotropic medications. I shudder to think of their plight if these medications were not available.

One of my sons has had suicide attempts and violent incidents with knives. He has also run out of our house—in a fit of terror—in subzero weather only to be found freezing and hypothermic by our local police department in the next township. These incidents all occurred when his illness was not adequately treated with antidepressant medication. My other son suffers from disabling obsessive-compulsive disorder symptoms and depression and has had his life improve dramatically from treatment with SSRIs.

Defending SSRIs

Many of my patients, as well as my children, have had severe symptoms from their illness that others may claim is from the treatment. I, as a mother and a psychiatrist, realize that the evidence linking suicidal behavior to SSRIs is weak and I will not draw conclusions lightly based on anecdotal information and isolated case reports. As a psychiatrist, I question whether some of the cases where a child worsened on SSRIs may have been because the child had bipolar disorder instead of unipolar depression. This has been posited by authorities in the field as well (American College of Neuropsychopharmacology Report to the FDA, dated January 21, 2004).

Upon review of the research, which confirms the experience of many NAMI families, NAMI believes that SSRI access for young people should be maintained.

The prevalence of mental illnesses in children and adolescents is significant and on the rise. Research shows that early identification and comprehensive treatment can improve the long-term prognosis of children with mental illnesses. Research on the effectiveness of treatments—including SSRIs and other psychotropic medications—is our best hope for the future.

With so many children and adolescents being prescribed psychotropic medications, we need research and science to help guide the safe and effective use of these medications. There is an essential need for more data on the long-term effects and safety of psychotropic medication use in children. NAMI calls on NIMH [National Institute of Mental Health] to make a significant investment in research on early onset mental disorders and the use of psychotropic medications—including SSRIs—for children and adolescents. This promises to help us understand the safety and effectiveness of SSRIs and other psychotropic medications in treating mental illnesses in children.

The discussion about children and adolescents and the use of SSRIs to treat depression must also address the critical need to ensure that all children and adolescents with mental illnesses have access to evidence-based assessments and interventions—with quality clinical care as an integral part of all aspects of the service delivery system. An expanded reporting system is necessary so that data from the pharmaceutical industry and other studies is available to the public.

Access to Psychiatric Medications Is Vital

For children with mental illnesses—especially those with persistent and serious mental illnesses—the ability to access psychiatric medications when needed is vital. NAMI believes that many children with mental illnesses need access to medication as part of a comprehensive treatment plan. NAMI is concerned that any limitations on the ability of knowledgeable practitioners to treat children with SSRIs, when needed, could be damaging to children in our country especially those with serious life altering illnesses.

Parents' or caregivers' decisions about whether to use SSRIs or other psychotropic medications for their child can be extremely difficult. Psychotropic medications for young children with mental illnesses should be used only when the anticipated benefits outweigh the risks. Parents and family members should be fully informed of the risks and expected benefits associated with medications prescribed for children and decisions about whether to use medication for a child should only be made after carefully weighing these factors. Children and adolescents who are taking psychotropic medications must be closely monitored and frequently evaluated by qualified mental health providers.

> **"** My children have had tremendous improvement with their illnesses and lead very full and functional lives because of SSRI medication. **"**

At the same time, psychotropic medications, including SSRIs, have been lifesaving for many children with mental illnesses. Families often report that the use of medication, either alone or along with other treatment modalities, has allowed their child to participate in school like other children, to live at home and to develop friendships with peers. We also know that the lack of effective treatment for a child or adolescent who needs it will adversely affect the child's overall physical and mental development, including the ability to learn, develop self-esteem, socialize and function in the community.

Dramatic Improvement

I have seen, along with many other clinicians, children respond positively to SSRIs—some dramatically. Moreover, there is little research on the outcomes that result from an absence of treatment, although lack of treatment undoubtedly leads to a greater number of preventable tragedies. SSRIs have actually been found to be effective in several recent reports while a large meta-analysis of an older alternative antidepressant family, the tricyclic antidepressants, failed to show the same improvements.

Another possible treatment alternative to SSRIs is cognitive-behavioral therapy (CBT), a form of psychotherapy. However, CBT has had a high treatment non-response rate for some children with depression, which provides yet another reason to have alternative treatments, like medications, available for children.

Many long-term studies show that the treatment of childhood onset depression with psychotherapy, medication or both improves the social and educational outcomes and emotional health of our children.

We are pleased that the FDA [Food and Drug Administration] is looking closely at the data related to SSRI use and suicidality. NAMI is deeply concerned with the public health crisis in the number of youth who commit suicide. We are also alarmed by the high number of youth with mental illnesses that fail to receive any treatment or services. The U.S. Surgeon General reports that up to 80% of youth who need mental health treatment fail to receive any treatment.

Tragic Consequences

NAMI families are well aware of the tragic consequences of untreated mental illnesses in youth. Suicide is the third leading cause of death in adolescents aged 15 to 24. Evidence strongly suggests that as many as 90% of those who commit suicide have a diagnosable mental disorder.

> *For children with mental illnesses . . . the ability to access psychiatric medications when needed is vital.*

Youth with untreated mental illnesses also tragically end up in jails and prisons—research shows that 65% of boys and 75% of girls in juvenile detention have at least one psychiatric diagnosis. They fail or drop out of school—leading to a greatly diminished future as citizens and productive workers.

Educators have found that children with a mental health disability—including depression—are most likely to flounder in the educational system and have lifelong complications from the lack of education if not adequately treated for their depressive symptoms. The risk of conduct problems and addictive behavior increases dramatically if any person with mental illness is not adequately treated.

Families across the country also struggle with accessing

mental health treatment for their child because of the crisis in the shortage of child and adolescent mental health providers—especially child-trained psychiatrists. The importance of a strong relationship between families and clinicians cannot be overstated; it is especially imperative in cases involving children and adolescents with depression.

The tragic reality is that the shortage of child and adolescent psychiatrists in this country—especially in rural communities—makes it extremely difficult for families to access appropriate and effective treatment for their child with a mental illness. These issues must be considered in the context of this discussion on the safety and efficacy of SSRIs to treat children and adolescents with depression.

More Studies Are Needed

In summary, I would like to thank the committee for allowing NAMI to share our views on these critically important issues. The families that we represent from across the country call for increased research and data to understand the long- and short-term safety and efficacy of SSRIs to treat children and adolescents with depression. Let us not forget that medications have been shown to be effective and no studies have proven that SSRIs cause suicide or suicidal behavior in young people. In fact, data suggest that SSRI use may have decreased suicides among young people, which is a critical public health problem.

NAMI is aware that not all of the data concerning the impact of SSRIs in children and adolescents has been made available to the public and independent researchers. It is critical that all such data be made available so that families everywhere can make decisions about treatment based on full knowledge of the risks and benefits. But we cannot stop there. Even if families and clinicians could make fully informed decisions about the use of SSRIs in a child, many families do not have access to providers. Services are woefully inadequate around the nation. And the current state of knowledge is simply inadequate—we need to understand mental illnesses in children much better and we need better treatments. If the FDA and U.S. federal government truly care about the well-being of American children with mental illnesses, it would address all of these issues.

12

People Are Overdiagnosed and Overmedicated for Depression

Ronald W. Dworkin

Ronald W. Dworkin is a practicing physician and an adjunct senior fellow at the Hudson Institute.

Since the early 1990s depression has been increasingly diagnosed, and antidepressants increasingly prescribed to combat it. Some doctors prescribe antidepressant medication for mere unhappiness because it is easier than taking the time to determine whether or not the patient is truly depressed. As a result, there is no longer a clear definition of clinical depression, and many patients who are just sad leave the doctor's office with drugs. The danger in medicating patients for everyday unhappiness is that the drugs do not solve problems, they just dull the senses. For this reason, antidepressants should not be used to treat everyday unhappiness but should be reserved solely for the treatment of clinical depression.

The use of psychotropic medication in depressed patients has increased in the United States by more than 40 percent over the last decade [since 1990], from 32 million office visits resulting in a drug prescription to over 45 million. This is in marked contrast to the period between 1978 and 1987, when the number of office visits resulting in a psychotropic drug pre-

Ronald W. Dworkin, "The Medicalization of Unhappiness," *Public Interest*, Summer 2001. Copyright © 2001 by National Affairs, Inc. Reproduced by permission of the publisher and the author.

scription remained relatively stable. The bulk of the increase can be accounted for by the aggressive use of SSRIs (selective serotonin reuptake inhibitors) in patients. It is the class of drugs that includes Prozac, Zoloft, and Paxil. The question is: Are more Americans clinically depressed now than in the past, or has medical science started to treat the far more common experience of "everyday unhappiness" with medication, thereby increasing the number of drug prescriptions?

Depression Is Now Diagnosed More Frequently

No one knows the answer to this question. We do know that the number of patients diagnosed with depression has doubled over the last 30 years, without any great change in diagnostic criteria. But this simply raises another question: Are doctors more aggressive in diagnosing depression, or are they simply diagnosing "everyday unhappiness" as a variant of depression and reporting it as such?

These questions are at the center of a major debate within the medical community over who the new patients being treated with antidepressants are and what treatment guidelines are being used. There is suspicion among some doctors that it is not the sickest patients who are being given psychotropic drugs but those patients who complain the loudest about being unhappy. Some physicians blame managed care for the problem of over-prescription. Because the office environment under managed care is so rushed and impersonal, many doctors take the path of least resistance by prescribing medication whenever a patient is feeling "blue." Also, managed-care companies save money when depressed patients receive medication rather than an indefinite number of counseling sessions.

> *There is suspicion among some doctors that it is not the sickest patients who are being given psychotropic drugs but those patients who complain the loudest about being unhappy.*

This suspicion is well founded, but the origin of the problem does not lie solely in managed care. The sources of overprescription are much more complex. Physicians are being encouraged to think about everyday unhappiness in ways that make them more likely to treat it with psychotropic medication. It is part of a growing phenomenon in our society: the medicalization of unhappiness.

In the past, medical science cared for the mentally ill, while everyday unhappiness was left to religious, spiritual, or other cultural guides. Now, medical science is moving beyond its traditional border to help people who are bored, sad, or experiencing low self-esteem—in other words, people who are suffering from nothing more than life.

This trend first became widely known with the publication in 1992 of *Listening to Prozac*. [Psychiatrist] Peter Kramer's book, which became a national best-seller, described the positive benefits enjoyed by depressed patients when they were put on Prozac. The drug apparently increased self-esteem and reduced negative feelings when nothing else could. The book led many in the medical community and the broader public to look more favorably on a liberal use of antidepressants.

> *Medical science errs when it supposes that a connection exists between everyday unhappiness and clinical depression.*

Medical science should aggressively use drugs like Prozac for patients suffering from clinical depression. This is totally appropriate—and important. But medical science errs when it supposes that a connection exists between everyday unhappiness and clinical depression, something it increasingly does. It is hard to know where everyday unhappiness ends and clinical depression begins, and there is no easy way to distinguish between borderline depression (i.e., low spirits without any physical signs or symptoms) and everyday unhappiness. Traditionally, doctors have relied on their wisdom, intuition, and personal experience to separate the two. Such a method is neither precise nor foolproof, but it is possibly the best we can aspire to. The problem is that medical science has placed everyday unhappiness and depression on a single continuum, thereby interfering with the efforts of doctors to make fine but necessary distinctions.

Medical science has adopted a method of classifying mental

disorders that blurs the line between sickness and health. And more radically, it has embraced a theory that explains all mental states in terms of their biochemical origins. Medical science has done this in order to make the problem of unhappiness simpler and more comprehensible to doctors. But the new science actually works against the efforts of doctors to separate everyday unhappiness from depression. The upshot is that physicians are more likely to treat mere unhappiness the way they would treat serious mental illness—with psychotropic drugs. . . .

While Kramer's *Listening to Prozac* examined the effects of Prozac on patients who were clinically ill, new research focuses on the effects of Prozac and other SSRIs on everyday unhappiness. According to medical science, the normal spectrum of individual differences in mood and social behavior may be tied to the same mechanism of neurotransmission that governs real mental pathology. One study postulates that different components of the human personality may have their own neurochemical substrates. These unique substrates, such as dopamine and serotonin—the same substrates involved in the biochemistry of clinical depression—may modulate the expression of everyday happiness and sadness.

Physicians have this theory in the back of their minds when they see depressed patients. They admit that depression may have many causes, but they still insist that moods are ultimately determined at the neuronal junctions of the brain where antidepressants work. In their view, all unhappiness necessarily leads back to these junctions in the same way that all roads once led to Rome.

This mindset prepares the way for a broad use of antidepressants. . . .

Is This Happiness?

The neuronal junctions of the brain where psychotropic drugs exert their effect are looked upon by medical science as a kind of corridor between matter and mood. Here at the subcellular level, the mystery of the human mood is believed to play itself out. A quantum of neurotransmitters is released at the neuronal junctions and a person's mood either rises or flags. The feeling of happiness gains an absolute unit of measurement in medical science and becomes, for all practical purposes, a visible phenomenon.

The flaw in this theory can be understood in the following

way: Matter and mood are two different phenomena, as different as light and air, and so can have no physical interface. Just as light and air cannot affect one another, since there is no place in the universe where they "meet," neither can matter and mood affect one another, since there is no place in the physical world where they meet. One is finite, the other is infinite; the two are composed of different substances and so can never be joined together in physical reality.

> **“[Antidepressants] are merely another form of stupefaction. ”**

It is true that neuronal junctions exist in the brain and that complex changes occur within these junctions during mental activity. But this does not necessarily make them a place where matter and mood share a common boundary. To say that they do is like watching a person get into a car, then seconds later watching the car move, and from this observation making the deduction that the car moves because someone gets into it. It is a false science to infer from the study of matter a knowledge any deeper than that of knowing the forms of matter and their relationships. It is a false science to say that on the basis of material knowledge, one can pretend to "know" and understand the emotional experience of life.

Kramer suggests that feelings like homesickness or loneliness are mediated through neurotransmitters like serotonin, or possibly encoded in neurons, and the fact that Prozac eases these conditions seems to confirm this view. But the notion that matter and mood can have a direct connection with one another—that somewhere at the neuronal junction, loneliness and serotonin "meet"—is tantamount to saying that the human mood is material, and that it can be touched by matter. Buried within the biogenic amine theory is an illogical belief— that neurotransmitters are shedding their physical existence, becoming even smaller than atoms, and ultimately merging with pure thought or idea.

The error in the biogenic amine theory can be understood in a slightly different way. [Christian philosopher Saint] Augustine once said that the human heart has more moods and emotions than hairs on the head or stars in the sky. What he meant by this is that happiness has an infinite number of shades, reflecting the infinite that is the human soul, which mirrors the infinite that is God. Even if every particle of serotonin crossing the synaptic cleft of a nerve terminal could be measured, along with every particle of noradrenalin and dopamine, the number of particles would still be finite, while the moods of a human being would still be infinite. By definition, there are simply not enough particles to express every conceivable human mood.

Creating Virtual Realities

But what about drugs like alcohol or narcotics? They alter our moods when ingested, producing feelings like euphoria and indifference. Is this not a case of matter affecting mood by way of a common border inside the brain?

No, it is not, and this is key to understanding how drugs like antidepressants really work. Alcohol and narcotics do not produce such feelings by being received directly into the "substance" of human emotions. On the contrary, they simply alter human consciousness in a way that allows the mind to shift its mood. These drugs work by dampening certain aspects of brain function—they create an altered mental state—such that true reality becomes concealed from a person's consciousness. The dampened brain functions allow a person to imagine an alternate "reality" that is generally more pleasing.

For example, when a man contrasts his humble circumstances with some ideal of success, tension arises in his psyche. His conscience berates him, and he feels the well-known misery of failure. He might try some diversion, like golf or stamp-collecting, in order to hide from himself what he does not want to face, but sometimes the diversion does not sufficiently block the sight of things that he dislikes. So he starts to drink, and the alcohol alters his consciousness in such a way that he is diverted. After ingesting alcohol, the eye of his mind no longer sees the images that were causing him so much pain. At this point, the man starts to feel better, even "happier."

Drinking is a reliable method of dealing with unhappiness not because it exerts a direct effect on a person's mood but because it helps conceal from view what he does not want to see. It is by dampening or altering brain functions and by affecting consciousness that alcohol transforms how we feel.

It is the same with antidepressants. They are merely another form of stupefaction. True, people who take them because they are unhappy are not like alcoholics or drug addicts—they function at work, they are well mannered, and they do not vomit in the streets. But although their method is "cleaner," they are attempting the same thing as the person who uses alcohol to raise his spirits. Unlike the drunk, their minds remain awake, clear, and lucid, but the drugs have still tampered with their brain functions, hiding from them what they do not want to see.

This point was revealed to me in the case of one friend who was taking Prozac for general unhappiness, though not under my supervision. He said, "I feel a lot better. I don't have to look into the abyss anymore. I see my problems, but they don't seem as daunting as they once did." With the help of a psychoactive drug, he was able to retire further and further from his mind's sight those images that were painful to him. He still saw their visible outlines, but his new mood was based on an altered perception of their image. He was no longer menaced by them because they had grown distant to him.

> " People . . . want to believe that the cause of happiness is located in the physical world, and that happiness somehow comes about scientifically in the form of a pill. "

The same phenomenon can account for what Kramer calls "cosmetic psychopharmacology." Kramer reports with amazement how one of his female patients, after taking Prozac, changed from a social misfit into an accomplished coquette, capable of maneuvering smoothly from one man to the next, even of securing three dates in a single weekend. But is this any different from what alcohol might do for someone with similar hesitations? Is this really a "new self" courtesy of Prozac? Of course not. A woman wants to flirt with men, but her self-doubt tells her not to do so. The result is tension and unhappiness. So she takes alcohol in order to silence the critic within and feel "liberated." This is nothing new.

Prozac Nation

Yet despite the rather obvious nature of antidepressants, medical science studiously avoids putting antidepressants in the same category as alcohol and narcotics. It struggles to preserve the deceit of a special mood-matter link at the level of the neuronal junctions. Why is this so? Why does it bother to support the irrational notion that mood and matter share a common interface? To the degree that it is a conspiracy, it is one enjoined by our entire culture: People desperately want to believe in such a link; they want to believe that the cause of happiness is located in the physical world, and that happiness somehow comes about scientifically in the form of a pill. The promise of such a view is security and comfort.

> *Medical science should confine itself to the treatment of clinical depression, rather than extend itself into the realm of everyday unhappiness.*

First, to admit one's dependence on psychoactive drugs is to shield oneself from life's imponderables and unpredictability. If happiness is serotonin, and serotonin is happiness, then these drugs guarantee happiness, for one can take psychoactive drugs for years. It is with this attitude that people with mild depression might substitute the chance of real happiness with some semblance of happiness achieved through medication.

Second, to declare happiness a law of necessity allows science to emphasize the subcellular processes inside the brain at the expense of everything else. Science can say: "It is man's basic nature to want happiness, but if the natural desire for happiness is linked to the physical nature of his brain, it cannot be linked to culture, which varies from society to society. The search for happiness begins and ends in nature, and so there is no reason to go beyond science." By believing this to be true, people can put aside other approaches to coping with daily troubles—which is convenient, since these remedies, whether they involve talking to a friend or asking for divine guidance, are never a sure thing.

Third, the notion that happiness is a law of science appeals to human pride. If unhappiness is chemical or biological, along with its treatment, a person need not ask, "Why am I unhappy?" In the past, this question provoked serious introspection and self-examination, as the effort to cope with unhappiness merged with larger questions about life and existence. Religion and philosophy demanded that people see themselves as part of a larger whole and taught that happiness depended on more than self-satisfaction. But if happiness is a law of science, then one does not have to go through this humbling experience. Through drugs, one can find happiness as a single, isolated individual.

Fourth, and perhaps most crucial, depressed persons equate the pleasant mood evoked by psychoactive drugs with happiness, even though, in the depths of their hearts, they are not sure exactly what they feel. Still, people do not want to live a lie, and so they will accept their drug-induced "happiness" as the real thing only if they believe that science has truly uncovered the biology of happiness. And this is what the biogenic amine theory of matter and mood represents. It reassures people who take medication that their good feeling is indeed happiness.

For people suffering from clinical depression, the mental state produced by these drugs must be considered an improvement, and often, a necessary one. But for those people who suffer from unhappiness, perhaps because of stress or because they are in bad relationships, these drugs are nothing more than a shortcut to a particular mental state that they believe to be happiness but is not.

Your Mind on Drugs

People medicated for depression often talk about enjoying activities that they did not enjoy prior to starting medication. But again, there is something suspicious in their pleasure. For example, two friends of mine told me that they "felt better" on medication, which enabled them to play tennis and feel good again while doing so. Yet it was not so much that they extracted pleasure from playing tennis but, rather, brought the pleasure they enjoyed through medication into this activity. It was a pleasure that they experienced for no discernible reason, and it mildly confused them since, deep down, they were the type of people who felt good only when external circumstances were going their way. Yet nothing in their lives had changed but a pill.

It has been observed that people who are not depressed and who take psychoactive drugs sometimes feel uncomfortable. The above observation might explain this phenomenon. The mood of such people is altered by drugs, but in a way that they cannot understand. They become like the traveler in a boat who feels confused by the imperceptible changes beneath his feet, and worse, has no beacon on the horizon on which to fix his gaze. He cannot establish a connection between what he is feeling and what he is seeing, so he starts to feel queasy. Nothing in the outer world seems to move, and so he cannot ascribe his inner feeling to an outside event. And if he does find a beacon sitting on the horizon, he cannot readily admit to himself, "Yes, I feel this way because of what I see," since what he sees never produced a feeling like this before. The whole thing makes no sense, and so he starts to feel seasick.

Know Thyself

Psychoactive medication, much like alcohol and narcotics, causes a disconnect between the inner and outer life. This is the problem with using it to treat everyday unhappiness. The disconnect caused by medication is very different from the state of thoughtful detachment encouraged by many cultures for the purpose of insulating people from everyday disappointment. The latter contributes to wisdom, stability, and maturity; the former creates a state of mind that is stuporous and purposely unknowing.

Medical science should confine itself to the treatment of clinical depression, rather than extend itself into the realm of everyday unhappiness. Medical science "helps" unhappy people by clouding their thoughts, by making them less aware of the world, and by sapping their urge to see themselves in a true light. People medicated for everyday unhappiness gain inner peace, but they do so through a real decrement in consciousness.

13

People Are Underdiagnosed and Undermedicated for Depression

Michael Simpson

Michael Simpson is a psychiatrist who works for MSN's Health24, a South African health content Web site aimed at promoting a greater understanding of health issues.

Too often, doctors overlook the problem of depression, diagnosing depressed patients as having only mild depression or failing to recognize the symptoms of depression at all. In addition, patients are frequently treated with doses of antidepressants that are too low to have an effect. As a result, doctors may switch their patients from drug to drug without waiting long enough to see if any one drug is actually working. Depression needs to be taken seriously by doctors and treated with appropriate dosages of antidepressants. Failure to do so results in many patient suicides.

"My GP [general practitioner] said it is only a mild depression, so I only need a small dose of a mild antidepressant."

I often hear this sort of comment, and it makes me shudder, as it represents a very serious problem which prevents many people from getting proper treatment for their depression. Let's run through the many problems included in such a statement.

First, there's a common misunderstanding of the nature of depression itself, and the person in this situation may not be significantly depressed at all. Depression is one of the commonest human afflictions. It is serious, it hurts and it has a significant death rate (mainly from suicide); a death rate rather higher than that of many other diseases which are treated more seriously by everyone.

> *"Depression is one of the commonest human afflictions. It is serious, it hurts and it has a significant death rate."*

In some ways, it's unfortunate that the disorder has come to have such a simple name: "depression", rather than an impressive technical term—or it might get more respect. Depression is a word, like anxiety, which is in common use for a wide range of states including depression, but also many milder, more transient situations—such as the blues, feeling down in the dumps, sad, disgruntled, disappointed, displeased, unhappy, cheerless, gloomy, downcast and so on.

Major Depression

The presence of so many terms, in most languages, for such negative moods, shows how common they are. But the sort of serious depression that needs serious treatment, goes beyond these (while often including all of them) and involves a range of biochemical changes in one's brain function.

Indeed, some specialists talk of a "biochemical depression" in order to make the distinction. All these other, lesser, mood states deserve respect and concern, but they are significantly different in degree and in significance.

What makes a major depression a significant illness rather than these unpleasant but briefer and more shallow moods, is the depth, extent and duration of the change in mood, and the extent of its effects on normal functioning.

Depression certainly features a severe degree of depressed mood, though some people seriously affected by it experience the other symptoms more severely and may not even recognise their state as depression.

The criteria which specialists and doctors use to diagnose depression look for this miserable mood to be present for most of the day, nearly every day. All normal people have variations in their mood, and it dips clown for some of the time. But that isn't depression.

Closely related to this is another criterion we look for, and one that is often even more reliable in indicating the presence of a real depression: a markedly diminished interest in whatever usually interests you, a loss of pleasure in what usually pleases you (technically called anhedonia).

The state should represent a real change from someone's previous state and not arising from an obvious immediate cause such as the death of a loved one (though depression can arise in the course of a bereavement); and it causes functional impairment: you are significantly less able to function as well as you usually do.

> *Many research studies and surveys have found that a great many patients in general practice are receiving far too little of [an antidepressant drug] to be able to benefit from it.*

There are several other features common in depression, which people often do not recognise as related, such as fatigue and loss of energy, difficulty in concentrating and making decisions, and feelings of being unworthy, and guilty, far in excess of anything that might be a reasonable response to events.

In a number of areas of functioning, the symptoms may swing in either direction—one may have insomnia, or sleep excessively, still not feeling refreshed by it. There can be increase in appetite and weight gain, or loss of appetite and weight loss; and one may become agitated and restless, or retarded and slowed down. Commonly, also, there are recurrent thoughts of death and futility, and thoughts of suicide.

This, then, is Depression with a Capital D, and the situation in which antidepressant drugs can be very useful, indeed lifesaving. While Depression can vary in severity, unless it is severe enough to meet the set of criteria specialists use to make the diagnosis, it is not severe enough to benefit from antidepressant therapy at all.

Too often, when the doctor says you have a "mild depression" he is hedging his bets. He is not really convinced whether the problem is severe enough to need serious and proper treatment. Far too often, he then talks of giving a minor or mild dose of an antidepressant drug.

Drugs Must Be Used Properly

Now comes the second problem. One must either use the antidepressant drug properly and in a sufficient dose to have a significant impact on correcting the biochemical abnormalities that have arisen in the depression; or not use it at all.

For each such drug, there is a minimum dose below which it will not produce any benefits. Lower doses may well give nasty side effects and even some risks, without any risk of benefiting the patient. It is simply an expensive and unpleasant way of taking needless risks.

Many research studies and surveys have found that a great many patients in general practice are receiving far too little of the drug to be able to benefit from it. Some of the people who say they have been treated with antidepressants, but without feeling better, fall into this category.

Doctors also often fail to wait long enough to see if a drug is working. Effective antidepressants may help to improve some aspects of your depression even earlier, but generally need a good two weeks to make a substantial difference to your condition.

> *Some doctors who were never well trained in psychiatry when in medical school don't take depression seriously enough.*

Too often, as a specialist, I see someone referred to me who has been given almost every antidepressant drug known to medical science, but who has had none of them in a sufficient dose or for a sufficient period. They might, in fact, respond excellently to any of those drugs, but have usually so thoroughly lost faith and confidence in that possibility, as to make their treatment needlessly difficult.

I also, too often, see patients whose depression has been treated with drugs which have no useful antidepressant effect, like the Valium family of tranquillisers. Such chemicals can even worsen a depression and increase one's impulsivity, which can be dangerous—just as alcohol, self-administered by many people in an effort to find a way to feel better, can have the same unfortunate effects.

Side Effects

Some drugs, especially the older antidepressants, have more side effects, and one may very well start on a rather low dose, and gradually increase it to the effective level.

This is fine, so long as the process is supervised by a doctor who knows what she is doing, and so long as the effective blood levels of the drug are reached.

> *There are frightening statistics from several research studies showing how many people saw their own doctor in the month before killing themselves, often within their last week of life.*

Newer antidepressants have less noticeable side effects, and can even be started at a potentially effective dose from the start. One may need to tolerate some degree of side effects, and accept them as a sign that the drug is getting to the right places and also doing what you want it to be doing.

A medication that is totally free of side effects would probably be just as free of effects and benefits, as well. Even a placebo (a dummy medication, consisting of starch, sugar pills or an injection of sterile water) usually also has side effects. In drug trials, using a placebo in comparison with an active drug, some patients complain bitterly of the side effects of the placebo, even stopping the non-existent drug, calling it intolerable.

Depression Often Not Noticed

Some doctors who were never well trained in psychiatry when in medical school don't take depression seriously enough. They may not recognise it when they see it.

Depression often acts as an amplifier of any other symptoms one has, making them feel worse and harder to tolerate.

Thus, depressed patients often go to see their doctor with other complaints at the top of their list (and doctors are often in such a hurry that they never let you tell them more than the top one or two complaints on your list).

> **❝** *In a very real and important sense, there is no such thing as that 'mild depression'. If it's really mild, it isn't depressing.* **❞**

We find a very high incidence of treatable and curable depression among patients at general medical or surgical outpatients departments or in medical or surgical hospital wards. Depression which amplifies pain may worsen someone's complaints about a relatively unimportant problem and lead to them being wheeled in for surgery, which will not solve their major problem.

Depression can be sneaky, either coming on so gradually that you don't really notice how severely it is affecting you before you are fully in its grip; or developing relatively rapidly, so that the tiredness, indecisiveness and hopelessness it causes within you, lead you to be inactive, give up and not take action to see a suitable professional who can help you get better.

Depression Influences Way of Thinking

The effect depression has on your way of thinking can be profound and dangerous. It fosters feelings of helplessness and hopelessness, as well as a feeling that you are only being a nuisance and really don't deserve to be helped. All these feelings are false and inaccurate—but dreadfully sincere, convincing, and seductive.

Research has shown the extent to which a depressed person, without realising it, selectively ignores the good news of the day and discounts anything hopeful, while selectively focusing on everything that is potentially bad news, gloomy and discouraging.

It's a perfect recipe for getting and staying more depressed. This is why, as well as drug treatment which is so effective in so many people, some specific types of psychotherapy such as so-called cognitive-behavioural therapies, can also be most useful.

The effect of these changes in one's way of perceiving the world and in evaluating one's situation, is to increase the danger of suicide. It is important to say that neither one's own thoughts of suicide, nor anyone else's "threats" or discussions of the subject, should ever be lightly ignored or discarded—all need to be carefully considered and the degree of risk assessed.

That's the other, often terribly final, reason why I feel a chill when hearing about someone's depression being lightly dismissed or treated with tiny doses of perhaps the wrong drug. Far, far too many people have died because of such failures.

There are frightening statistics from several research studies showing how many people saw their own doctor in the month before killing themselves, often within their last week of life. There, surely, could have been a real chance to recognise the situation and to deal with it effectively.

General practitioners and other doctors, as well as mental health workers, have a major responsibility to consider the possibility of the presence of a significant degree of depression and of suicide risk when they see and assess patients, whatever the person is "officially" complaining about.

If they find a good reason to diagnose depression, they must see that the person gets an effective dose of an effective treatment.

These drugs are not like salt, something you can simply sprinkle over someone, to an individual taste. Either they are used effectively, or there is no point in using them at all. In fact, the ineffective and feeble doses so popular among some GPs probably increase the danger.

Because they cannot work effectively, they may add the burden of pointless side effects and convince the person that, as the treatment is not working, their situation may be hopeless, when this is not so.

The responsibility should also be shared by patients, friends and families.

If you are the depressed person, you have a responsibility to yourself and to those who care about you, so make sure that you see someone suitably trained, and that you reveal all aspects of how you feel, including thoughts of suicide where these are present. Friends and family should also encourage this.

Being depressed is usually no more your fault than is having appendicitis, so be frank and play as active a part as you can in your own recovery.

In a very real and important sense, there is no such thing as that "mild depression". If it's really mild, it isn't depressing.

Organizations to Contact

The editors have compiled the following list of organizations concerned with the issues debated in this book. The descriptions are derived from materials provided by the organizations. All have publications or information available for interested readers. The list was compiled on the date of publication of the present volume, the information provided here may change. Be aware that many organizations take several weeks or longer to respond to inquiries, so allow as much time as possible.

American Academy of Child and Adolescent Psychiatry
3615 Wisconsin Ave. NW, Washington, DC 20016-3007
(202) 966-7300 • fax: (202) 966-2891
Web site: www.aacap.org

The American Academy of Child and Adolescent Psychiatry is a professional medical organization made up of child and adolescent psychiatrists trained to promote healthy development and to evaluate, diagnose, and treat children and adolescents and their families who are affected by disorders of feeling, thinking, and behavior. It publishes the *Journal of the American Academy of Child and Adolescent Psychiatry*.

American Association of Suicidology
4201 Connecticut Ave. NW, Suite 408, Washington, DC 20008.
(202) 237-2280 • fax: (202) 237-2282
e-mail: amyjomc@ix.netcom.com • Web site: www.cyberpsych.org

The association is one of the largest suicide prevention organizations in the nation. It believes that suicidal thoughts are usually a symptom of depression and that suicide is rarely a rational decision. The association provides referrals to regional crisis centers in the United States and Canada and helps those grieving the death of a loved one.

American Psychiatric Association (APA)
1400 K St. NW, Washington DC 20005
(202) 682-6000 • fax: (202) 682-6850
e-mail: apa@psych.org • Web site: http://psych.org

The APA is an organization of psychiatrists dedicated to studying the nature, treatment, and prevention of mental illnesses such as depression. The APA helps create mental health policies, distributes information about psychiatry, and promotes psychiatric research education. It publishes the *American Journal of Psychiatry* and *Psychiatric Services* monthly.

American Psychological Association (APA)
750 First St. NE, Washington, DC 20002-4242
(202) 336-5500 • fax: (202) 336-5708
e-mail: public.affairs@apa.org • Web site: www.apa.org

This society of psychologists aims to "advance psychology as a science, as a profession, and as a means of promoting human welfare." APA seeks to promote knowledge of illnesses like depression through meetings, professional contacts, and the publication of reports and papers. It produces numerous publications, including the monthly journal *American Psychologist*, the monthly newspaper *APA Monitor*, and the quarterly *Journal of Abnormal Psychology*.

Canadian Mental Health Association
8 King St. E., Suite 810, Toronto, ON M5C 1B5 Canada
(416) 484-7750 • fax: (416) 484-4617
e-mail: national@cmha.ca • Web site: www.cmha.ca

The Canadian Mental Health Association is one of the oldest voluntary organizations in Canada. Its programs are designed to assist people suffering from mental illness such as depression, helping them to cope with crises, regain confidence, and return to their communities, families, and jobs. It publishes books, reports, policy statements, and pamphlets.

Depression and Bipolar Support Alliance (DBSA)
730 N. Franklin St., Suite 501, Chicago, IL 60610-7204
(800) 826-3632 • fax: (312) 642-7243
Web site: www.dbsalliance.org

The Depression and Bipolar Support Alliance is the nation's leading patient-directed organization focusing on the most prevalent mental illnesses: depression and bipolar disorder. The organization fosters an understanding about the impact and management of these illnesses by providing up-to-date, scientifically based tools and information written in a language the general public can understand. DBSA supports research to promote more timely diagnoses, develop more effective and tolerable treatments, and discover a cure for these illnesses. The organization also works to ensure that people living with mood disorders are treated equitably. It publishes several books, including *How I Stayed Alive When My Brain Was Trying to Kill Me*, as well as several brochures about bipolar disorder and suicide.

National Alliance for Research on Schizophrenia and Depression (NARSAD)
60 Cutter Mill Rd., Suite 404, Great Neck, NY 11021
(516) 829-0091 • fax: (516) 487-6930
e-mail: info@narsad.org • Web site: www.narsad.org

The alliance is a nonprofit coalition of citizens' groups that raises funds for research into the causes, treatments, cures, and prevention of severe mental illnesses. It publishes *NARSAD Research*, a quarterly newsletter.

National Alliance for the Mentally Ill (NAMI)
Colonial Place Three, 2107 Wilson Blvd., Suite 300, Arlington, VA 22201
(703) 524-7600 • fax: (703) 524-9094
Web site: www.nami.org

NAMI is a consumer advocacy and support organization composed largely of family members of people with severe mental illnesses, including depression. The alliance adheres to the position that mental illnesses are biological brain diseases and that people suffering from depression should not be blamed or stigmatized for their condition. Its publications include the bimonthly newsletter *NAMI Advocate* and the book *Breakthroughs in Antipsychotic Medications.*

National Foundation for Depressive Illness (NAFDI)
PO Box 2257, New York, NY 10116
(800) 239-1265
Web site: www.depression.org

NAFDI provides information about depression and manic-depressive illness. It promotes the view that these disorders are physical illnesses treatable with medication, and it believes that such medication should be made readily available to those who need it. The foundation publishes the quarterly newsletter *NAFDI News* and the fact sheet "Symptoms of Depression and Manic Depression."

National Institute of Mental Health (NIMH)
6001 Executive Blvd., Room 8184, Msc 9663, Bethseda, MD 20892-9663
(301) 443-4513 • fax: (301) 443-4279
e-mail: nimhinfo@nih.gov • Web site: www.nimh.gov

NIMH is the federal agency concerned with mental health research. It plans and conducts a comprehensive program of research relating to the causes, prevention, diagnosis, and treatment of mental illness. It produces various informational publications on mental disorders and their treatment.

National Mental Health Association
1021 Prince St., Alexandria, VA 22314-2971
(703) 684-7722 • fax: (703) 684-5968
e-mail: nmhainfo@aol.com • Web site: www.nmha.org

The association is a consumer advocacy organization concerned with combating mental illness and improving mental health. It promotes research into the treatment and prevention of mental illness, monitors the quality of care provided to the mentally ill, and provides educational materials on mental illness and mental health. It publishes the monthly newsletter the *Bell* as well as various pamphlets and reports.

Obsessive-Compulsive Foundation (OCF)
676 State St., New Haven, CT 06511
(203) 401-2070 • fax: (203) 401-2076
e-mail: info@ocfoundation.org • Web site: www.ocfoundation.org

The foundation consists of individuals with obsessive-compulsive disorders (OCDs), their friends and families, and the professionals who treat them. It works to increase public awareness of, and discover a cure for, obsessive-compulsive disorders. It publishes the bimonthly *OCD Newsletter* and the pamphlet *OCD Questions and Answers.*

Bibliography

Books

William S. Appleton   *The New Antidepressants and Antianxieties: What You Need to Know About Prozac, Zoloft, Luvox, Wellbutrin, Effexor, Serzone, Vestra, Celexa, St. John's Wort, and Others.* New York: Penguin Group, 2004.

Jill S. Goldberg Arnold   *Raising a Moody Child: How to Cope with Depression and Bipolar Disorder.* New York: Guilford, 2003.

Samuel H. Barondes   *Better than Prozac: Creating the Next Generation of Psychiatric Drugs.* New York: Oxford University Press, 2003.

Peter R. Breggin   *Antidepressant Fact Book: What Your Doctor Won't Tell You About Prozac, Zoloft, Paxil, Celexa, and Luvox.* New York: Perseus, 2001.

Peter R. Breggin and David Cohen   *Your Drug May Be Your Problem.* New York: Perseus, 2000.

Joseph Glenmullen   *Prozac Backlash: Overcoming the Dangers of Prozac, Zoloft, Paxil, and Other Antidepressants with Safe, Effective Alternatives.* New York: Simon & Schuster, 2001.

David Healy   *Antidepressant Era.* Cambridge, MA: Harvard University Press, 1999.

David Healy   *Let Them Eat Prozac: The Unhealthy Relationship Between the Pharmaceutical Industry and Depression.* New York: New York University Press, 2004.

Harold S. Koplewicz   *More than Moody: Recognizing and Treating Adolescent Depression.* New York: Perigee Trade, 2003.

William A. McKim   *Drugs and Behavior.* Upper Saddle River, NJ: Prentice-Hall, 2003.

Andrew L. Morrison   *The Antidepressant Sourcebook: A User's Guide for Patients and Families.* New York: Doubleday, 2000.

Richard O'Connor   *Active Treatment of Depression.* New York: W.W. Norton, 2001.

Paul Raeburn   *Acquainted with the Night: A Parent's Quest to Understand Depression and Bipolar Disorder in His Children.* New York: Broadway Books, 2004.

Matthew Sharpe   *The Sleeping Father.* Brooklyn, NY: Soft Skull, 2003.

Andrew Solomon	*Noonday Demon: An Atlas of Depression.* New York: Simon & Schuster, 2001.
E. Fuller Torrey and Michael B. Knable	*Surviving Manic Depression: A Manual on Bipolar Disorder for Patients, Families, and Providers.* New York: Basic Books, 2002.
Carol Turkington and Eliot F. Kaplan	*Making the Antidepressant Decision.* Lincolnwood, IL: NTC, 2001.

Periodicals

Joseph Annibali	"Prozac on Trial—a Psychiatrist Argues That Misuse of Antidepressants Has Endangered Patients' Lives When Safer, More Natural Alternatives Are Available," *World & I*, September 2002.
Erika Check	"Antidepressants: Bitter Pills," *Nature*, September 8, 2004.
Rebecca A. Clay	"Psychotherapy Is Cost-Effective," *Monitor on Psychology*, January 2000.
Daniel DeNoon	"Group Finds No Suicide-Antidepressant Link," *WebMD Medical News*, January 21, 2004.
Hillel Grossman	"Misplacing Empathy and Misdiagnosing Depression: How to Differentiate Among Depression's Many Faces," *Geriatrics*, April 2004.
Harvard Mental Health Letter	"Interpersonal Psychotherapy," August 2004.
Harvard Mental Health Letter	"Should Children Take Antidepressants?" December 2003.
Harvard Women's Health Watch	"Treating Depression: Update on Antidepressants," June 2004.
Jeremy Hazlehurst	"Prozac's Downer," *Spiked-Health*, October 9, 2003.
Joli Jensen	"Emotional Choices: What You Choose to Believe About Antidepressants Reveals a Deeper Truth About Who You Are," *Reason*, April 2004.
Johns Hopkins Medical Institutions	"Antidepressants Plus 'Talk Therapy' Are Effective Therapy for Teen Depression," December 2004.
Kathiann M. Kowalski	"Are Antidepressants the Answer? The Number of Teens Taking Antidepressants Is on the Rise. Find Out What This Means," *Current Health 2*, October 2002.
Jeanne Lenzer	"Secret US Report Surfaces on Antidepressants in Children," *British Medical Journal*, August 7, 2004.
Tanya Luhrmann	"Learning from Prozac: Will New Caution Shift Old Views?" *New York Times*, March 30, 2004.
Apoorva Mandavilli	"Mood Swings," *Nature Medicine*, September 8, 2004.

Hara Estroff Marano   "Antidepressants: The Kid Question," *Psychology Today*, February 2004.

Hara Estroff Marano   "How to Take an Antidepressant: It's No Longer Enough to Treat Depression; It's Necessary to Banish It. What's the Best Drug for That? It Boils Down to What Side Effects You Can Tolerate in the Long Haul," *Psychology Today*, January/February 2003.

J.S. McNamara   "Antidepressants: Worth the Risks?" *Daily Texan*, March 8, 2004.

Michael E. Thase   "Small Effects Are Not Trivial from a Public Health Perspective," *Psychiatric Times*, September 2002.

Shankar Vedantam   "Antidepressant Makers Withhold Data," *Washington Post*, January 29, 2004.

Rob Waters   "Drug Report Barred by FDA Scientist Links Antidepressants to Suicide in Kids," *San Francisco Chronicle*, February 1, 2004.

Index